Newcastle Battalions
in action on the Somme

Neil Storey and Fiona Kay

Published by:
Newcastle Libraries, City of Newcastle Upon Tyne
Tyne Bridge Publishing, 2016
www.tynebridgepublishing.co.uk

Design: David Hepworth

Acknowledgements:

Neil Storey and Fiona Kay would like to thank: Lesley Freyter, Fusiliers Museum of Northumberland, Major Chester Potts T.D., Chairman of the Northumberland and North East Fusiliers Association, Keith Laws, Chairman Northumberland Royal British Legion, Alan Fidler, Northumbria World War One Commemoration Project, Billy Embleton, Jim Smith and Ian Johnson for their kind support, encouragement and help with this book.

Members of the 6th Battalion Northumberland Fusiliers (T.F.) at Gosforth Park, September 19...

Contents

A colourful and patriotic fold out postcard of views from Newcastle 1914.

Two of the Drummer boys of the 16th (Newcastle) Battalion, Northumberland Fusiliers 'Newcastle Commercials' 1914

Foreword

When we were growing up we were both privileged to have known the last few of that remarkable generation of men and women in our home towns who served in the First World War and most certainly knew many of those who lived through those turbulent times as kids on the home front.

The people of Newcastle and the North East have always had a quiet pride, warmth and dignity that is difficult to describe in words. It can be sensed and seen in so many ways by anyone, be they born and bred local or regular visitor alike, especially in the way a Geordie makes a wry observation or tells a story. That said there was a reticence among all those we knew to freely talk about The First World War and it was simply understood the men had done their bit and many just wanted to put it away as best they could remembering publicly once a year on Remembrance Sunday with maybe an occasional story, perhaps a funny one brought to mind by something they had seen or read, a story that may well tail off with a lingering look into the distance, remembering something more... in silence.

Now that generation has passed. With them went their memories and what is left in the popular recollections of what happened to our local lads in the First World War varies greatly. There are some really good battalion histories written shortly after the war, some have been written in more recent times too but even now there remain battalions where there is no

book to tell the story of how they were raised, where they trained, the characters who served in their ranks, what happened to them when they went into action, the battles they fought in and the heroes that emerged.

Our book does not pretend to be an authoritative account of all of them but more of a starting point, perhaps even a timely reminder. It is most certainly intended as a small tribute to the numerous battalions of volunteer soldiers raised in Newcastle before and during the First World War that were present on that fateful First Day of the Somme on 1 July and the ensuing days, weeks and months of the battle to the end of November 1916.

In their assessment of the Somme military historians point out that the battle marked a turning point in the war that broke the deadlock in the trenches and marked the beginning of the end of the war on the Western Front but no one will ever deny it did not come at a hell of a cost in killed and wounded. All those who passed through that crucible of war bore the mental scars of what they lived through to their dying day. Everyone in Newcastle lost someone special to them be they family or friend. Things were never quite the same again.

This book is dedicated to the memory of wor lads who fought on the Somme.

Neil Storey & Fiona Kay

The view from St. Mary's Church, Gateshead across the Tyne to Quayside and Newcastle c1910

Northumberland, Newcastle and its people in 1914.

By 1914, Great Britain's Empire spread across the world and had enjoyed the boom of the industrial revolution where factories, mines, ship yards, railways and increased mechanisation had transformed areas of the country into industrial powerhouses and Northumberland, England's most northern county was most certainly one of them.

In the *Kelly's* county trade directories of the early twentieth century, Northumberland was recorded as the fifth largest county of England with a population 'chiefly descended from the Northumbrian English of Northumberland, Durham and the Lowlands with a liberal dash of Scottish and Irish and very few immigrants from South or Middle England.'

Improvements in sanitation and healthcare during the nineteenth and early twentieth centuries had also helped to reduce child mortality and people here were living longer despite many folks being employed in hard industrial jobs in dangerous and unhealthy working conditions. Couple this with living in a county known for its cold and wet climate, a combination not usually associated with long life and good health and it is remarkable to find the population had increased to over five times its size since the beginning of the nineteenth century, recorded as 696,893 people in the county after the 1911 census. It should not be forgotten that

thousands were drawn to bring themselves and their families to the county over that time for the employment opportunities it offered but still it is clear that born and bred Northumbrians were hardy folk.

Deep below the fertile land of the county there were pits, quarries and excavations for iron and lead ore, barium, clay, limestone, sandstone and above all coal. A massive 13,381,641 tons of 'King Coal' was blasted and hewed from the seams in the county in 1912 alone, to power the engines that kept industry rolling, warmed our homes and fired the boilers of our steam engines on railways and in ships over the seven seas. In Northumberland in 1912 there were 128 collieries employing 48,450 men underground and 10,854 workers on the surface. The hub of it all was Newcastle, its Quayside was the centre of the British Empire's coal trade and its Commercial Exchange was the heart of that business.

There would be as many as five hundred people representing ship owners, ship brokers, coal exporters and colliery sales agents on the floor of the Exchange every morning and again in the afternoon. There was a telegraph office and ten telephone boxes. Trade would be conducted all over the world and to the young men entering the Exchange as clerks it seemed like the hub of the universe.

Quayside and 'Up Street' were the centre of the coal trade but in 1914 Newcastle's population of 266,603 were not only employed in coal there were also many 'white collar jobs' for aspiring young men. There were jobs in insurance, shipping, and newspapers, there were also shops and businesses aplenty as well as manual labour jobs in the municipal and public works, the North Eastern Railway, Corporation Tramways and utilities and of course there was ship building on the Tyne.

Shipbuilding was truly a great industry, both nationally and internationally. The Tyne was second only to the Clyde for ship building in the British Empire in 1914 and names such as the Wallsend Slipway and Engineering Company; Swan, Hunter & Wigham Richardson (with Yards at Low Walker and Wallsend) and Armstrong, Whitworth & Co employed thousands. Indeed, Armstrong's, the greatest of them all, not only had their own ordnance factory, steel works and shipyard on a seventy-two acre site at Elswick for the construction of warships where they employed some 22,000 men, they had another yard for mercantile vessels at Walker and a further works at Scotswood to build motor cars and wagons. The net tonnage of the shipping launched from Newcastle in 1912 amounted to 121,854 tons of British vessels and 37,357 tons for foreign trade.

Despite all of this industry there were still those out of work. Some sought regular employment by travelling across Britain to other cities and towns to find it. Others went far further afield by buying or working their passage abroad or if they were out of work there were schemes that granted men and their families passage to start new lives in British dominions or colonies such as Canada and Australia. While many other young, fit men, with hopes of seeking adventure and seeing the world walked to their nearest barracks and joined up in a Regular Army battalion of the grand old local Regiment – the 'Fighting Fifth' – The Northumberland Fusiliers.

Businesses commercial and clerical side by side on bustling Grainger Street, Newcastle c1910.

For King and Country

In the early twentieth century Regular soldiers had a good and active life serving their King and Country both at home and abroad and the men of the Northumberland Fusiliers were no exception. They were well fed, accommodated in barracks or under canvas in tents and would have a routine of parade ground drill, skill-at-arms, duties and exercises that kept the soldier's training fresh as well as a regular round of sports and games from running, swimming and boxing to rugby, football and even tug-of-war. They also had the benefit of the temperance associations within the military to maintain the good work of keeping soldiers sober. Army education was also well-established and Christian and friendly societies were encouraged. Indeed, the British soldier in India could live very well, even other ranks soldiers could take their family out there and afford to have servants – now that would have been a turn up for the boys from Wallsend. Although there were small campaigns there had been no major conflict since the Second Anglo-Boer War (1899-1902); these years of the Regular Army would often be recalled as the best of peace-time soldiering.

During the decade immediately before the First World War, the British Army was revolutionised by the reforms

Left: Band of 2nd Battalion, Northumberland Fusiliers at The Citadel, Dover, July 1908.
Above: Drummer Boy, 1st Battalion, Northumberland Fusiliers c1908

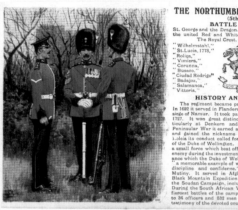

Left: The Drums, 1st Battalion, Northumberland Fusiliers decked with red and white roses for St. George's Day, Charial, India 1910 (FMN).
Above: One of the famous Gale & Polden History and Traditions Series for The Northumberland Fusiliers with artwork by Ernest Ibbetson c1910

enacted by Richard Burdon Haldane, the Liberal government's Secretary of State for War (1905-1912). The most significant of these was the complete reorganisation of the Home Field Army and Reserve System. Under this scheme most line infantry regiments would have two regular battalions, one was to provide garrison troops across the British Empire, in the case of the Northumberland Fusiliers there were foreign stations in India. The other Battalion would be based in Britain and Ireland on 'Home Service' and could be mobilized at short notice to form a British Expeditionary Force (B.E.F.) in the event of a war emergency. There was also an Army Reserve and a Special Reserve, most common of which were soldiers who had served their time but were held on record for five years as a Reservist.

Haldane got rid of the old Volunteer system in favour of a new Territorial Force of part-time soldiers who would train to defend the home territory in the event of a 'war emergency,' taking the place of the Regular battalions that would have been sent to Europe as a B.E.F.

Reflecting years later many of those who were young men when joining the Territorial Force in peacetime before the Great War acknowledged that their actions had been motivated by patriotism and a sense of duty. They were also fired up by the bravado of youth and fancied a smart uniform to impress the girls, but above all it was to share adventures and sports and experience a touch of the army life with their mates.

The requirements to join the Territorials stipulated men had to be aged between seventeen and thirty-five, with a minimum chest measurement of thrity-three inches, a minimum height of five foot two inches and a willingness to enlist for a minimum of four years in the Territorial Force. Upon joining, the recruit was obliged to attend forty drills in his first year of enlistment. In the Battalion one hour of two drill nights each week was set aside for 'square bashing' on the parade ground. A Territorial was also required to pass through a recruits' course of musketry held on two appointed afternoons through the summer months. In the second, third and fourth years of service the Recruit became a 'Trained Man,' obliged to perform twenty drills in the second year, ten drills in the third and fourth years and the Trained Man's Course of Musketry. Throughout this period there would be regular parades and weekend manoeuvres. Such exercises were often the butt of jokes among the roughs of a town or village and any recruit would soon find membership of the Territorial Force earned him the nickname of a 'Saturday Night Soldier.'

The experience of training was however something that forged a great deal of close comradeship between the men and their Officers as well as great pride in unit performance. Many of the Officers were men from local families of good standing, in professions such as solicitors, businessmen and white collar office managers at the local ship builders or collieries who had been raised in the tradition of not only leading their men but understanding them. Undoubtedly there was a strong element of deference but many officers gained the respect of their men through leading by example and demonstrating good military sense, discipline, training and even good humour when it really mattered.

Top: A prize winning football team from a Regular Army Battalion of the Northumberland Fusiliers c1910.
Right: A Captain and his NCO's from 6th (Newcastle) Battalion, Northumberland Fusiliers (T.F.)while on camp 1910.

The greater affluence of the new middle class in the nineteenth century also saw the unprecedented expansion and creation of grammar schools and new public schools. Public schools were the heartlands of the new generation of young men being prepared through education and tutorage to lead as managers, business directors and captains of industry and to aspire to be a new generation of ultra patriotic military leaders fit to be Officers *and* gentlemen. Haldane began to form his seed-bed of future military leaders by creating the Officers Training Corps in 1907. The movement had two divisions: 'Senior' based in the Universities and 'Junior' working in Public and Grammar schools but both working with the express aim of providing as many officers as possible for the Special Reserve and the new Territorial Force.

The War Office also recognised that in the event of a major European war, the existing medical arrangements for Britain's armed forces would be wholly inadequate. Some form of supplementary aid in addition to the Territorial Force Medical Service would be required to provide transport and care for the thousands of casualties returned from a British Expeditionary Force fighting on the Continent. The problem was training and maintaining such a force in peacetime when the demands upon the extant army medical services were not heavy. It was solved with a call for an all volunteer scheme, specifically the *Scheme for the Organisation of Voluntary Aid in England and Wales* issued on 16 August 1909. The British Red Cross Society and Order of St John, (although at that time working as separate Voluntary Aid Societies) immediately began to establish so-called Voluntary Aid Detachments (V.A.D.s) to

recruit and train local volunteers for the task. There were no mixed units, the men usually became stretcher bearers or ambulance sections while the women undertook nursing and hospital duties; very soon V.A.D. detachments were being established across Northumberland.

The children who were maturing to adulthood in the early twentieth century, had been a generation that had benefitted from the 1870 Foster Education Act. Having been schooled in the three 'R's of Reading, wRiting and aRithemtic they could look to a greater variety of employment opportunities than any generation before. Cross-country transport and international shipping could mean that the world, or at least the great British Empire was their oyster. But these children were different; they had not only been schooled in education, they had been educated in patriotism. Schools would often have flag poles and begin and end each day with a flag ceremony, the children would give thanks to the monarch in their prayers and with the empire at its zenith the children's text books and lessons would regularly include both overt and subtle references to it. Children's illustrated story papers such as the *Boy's Own Paper* and *Union Jack* were filled with tales of brave and patriotic young folk. School prize books by such authors as G. A. Henty, Captain F. S. Brereton and Rudyard Kipling hammered home this ethos with volumes swathed in suitably dramatic pictorial covers that told stories of derring do from English history and the exploits of the men who built and fought to defend the far flung outposts of the British Empire

With the patriotic ethos everywhere boys who did not attend the public schools where there were OTCs did

Clockwise from top left: 1) No. 4 (North Shields) Boy's Brigade Stretcher Bearer Section c1910. *2)* Members of the Church Lads Brigade learned rifle drill in the years before and during The First World War. 3)A Company of the Tyne Electrical Engineers, North Shields 1914. 4) Boy's Brigade Camp, Warkworth 1906.

not miss out on the chance to learn the skills required to be loyal and adventurous Britons. They were able to join such organisations as the Boy's Brigade and the Church Lad's Brigade that were uniformed, taught drill, discipline, skill at arms with rifles and even held camps run on military lines. Then there was the Boy Scout movement founded by national hero General Robert Baden Powell in 1907. The first Scout units in Northumberland emerged from 1908, indeed it was that same year that the first camp of trained Scouts assembled under Baden-Powell's leadership was held at Humshaugh. It was far from chance that the Boy Scouts, an organisation that epitomised and espoused the ideals for patriotic and dutiful boys, were listed directly under the military forces of the county in the 1914 *Kelly's Directory*. It was intended the Boy Scouts and Sea Scouts would provide the home forces with ready hands to help out, additional eyes to observe and to act as both signallers and messenger carriers on bicycles and on foot if there was to be a war.

4th Battalion, Northumberland Fusiliers (T.F.) on manoeuvres c1912.

14

Summer 1914

"The lamps are going out all over Europe, we shall not see them lit again in our life-time."

Sir Edward Grey of Fallodon, Secretary of Foreign Affairs, 3 August 1914

The summer of 1914 was truly magnificent, the sun blazed down and all who lived through it would look back on those halcyon days with the greatest affection despite the gathering clouds of war. There were all the usual features of summer back in those days when Arthur Laycock and the St. Hilda's Colliery band played at Leazes Park and the likes of Amers' or Smith's bands played in public spaces like Armstrong Park and the Recreation Ground on North Road. Even the Newcastle Glee and Madrigal Society performed al fresco rehearsals at the race course. The Hoppings and Durham Regatta in June were all well attended, as were the usual round of outdoor fetes that then featured hotly contested band competitions and sporting matches such as tug-of-war and slippery poles. There were also church bazaars, tea parties and charity fund raising events with street collections like Alexandra Rose Day, where hundreds of women dressed in fine white summer dresses thronged the principal thoroughfares rattling collection boxes and presenting finely made artificial roses in return for donations. Over £200 was raised, five per cent of which went to the hospitals and kindred institutions in London in which Queen Alexandra was personally interested, the remainder was devoted to providing for the aged poor of Newcastle.

It would, however, be wrong to paint a picture of a totally idyllic time, there were dark clouds at both home

The New Promenade at Whitley Bay during one of those long hot summers in the years just before the First World War.

NEW PROMENADE WHITLEY BAY

15

It's nice to have a "buoy" hanging round at WHITLEY BAY

I am merry and bright and full of delight,
And pleasures my hours surround,
But I feel fit to sing, and life goes with a swing,
When a boy is hanging around!

1097

A jolly greetings postcard from Whitley Bay in 1914.

and abroad in July 1914. A number of Northumbrian mines had reduced the hours for their miners, making times hard for their families; the future for South Tyne and Blackett Pits was far worse and their closure due in September threatened to put 1,000 men and boys out of work. A strike over pay and conditions was narrowly averted on the Newcastle Tramways and as the Women's Suffrage movement was becoming increasingly militant with demonstrations and damage to property occurring across the country, there was even a protest made by a Suffragette at Newcastle Cathedral. On the wider stage, the Home Rule crisis raged in Ireland and after the assassination of Archduke Franz Ferdinand of Austria on 29 June the newspapers increasingly filled their columns with reportage of 'the Sarajevo Crime' and its impact on diplomatic relationships and old alliances as the situation escalated into a crisis which saw European nations mobilise, troops concentrating on the frontiers and ultimately led to the outbreak of the First World War.

During that last month many people were determined to make the best of what was left of the summer of 1914, no matter what the future may hold. For many it was time to take a holiday or at least have a day trip to the seaside while they still could and the coastal resorts were enjoying a bumper season. Thousands had flocked to the seaside where they had a chance to sun themselves in deck chairs, roll up trouser legs and hitch up skirts to plodge in the water and perhaps take in a seaside show such as Pierrots or troubadours. On the railways day trippers and holidaymakers packed the trains for Whitley Bay while the departure of continental boat trains was marked by the absence of British and American travellers. Instead the grave faces of French, Italians, Spanish and Germans filled the compartments and the steamers from the continent were noted for carrying large numbers of German and Dutch women being sent to Britain for safety.

Sports such as horse racing, golf, tennis, cricket, and football friendlies were played right up to the eve of war. It had been good going for horse racing at Gosforth the 'Pitmen's Derby' for the Northumberland Plate had been run in June but it had been noted the attendance in the Members' Enclosure had been rather thin on account of the Officers from all services who would have usually been present having been called to duty, and this had also kept away their relatives and friends. It was observed, however, that those in the cheaper stands seemed to be making a bumper day of it, albeit that they too were fewer in number.

As ever, the local Territorial Force Battalions of the Northumberland Infantry Brigade had made the most of the summer by holding local manoeuvres, field days and their fifteen-day annual camp in June where they enjoyed good weather and activities in the magnificent countryside of Greystoke Camp, Penrith, Cumbria. The camp that year was made all the more interesting to the troops as it was shared with Territorial Royal Field Artillery units from the North Riding of Yorkshire, Scarborough and the Whitley Battery. They were also joined by the Royal Engineers from Newcastle.

The Voluntary Aid Detachments were also active, roping in local youth groups such as Boy Scouts and Church Lad's Brigade as runners and 'casualties' for their drills and exercises. Locally, Elswick was 'attacked by a Foreign Power' in July 1914 and remarkable scenes were enacted during the exercise in Walker where twenty-five casualties represented by the Boy's Life Brigade were treated by No.11 (Walker) and No. 52 (Jesmond Ladies) Northumberland Voluntary Aid Detachments, the latter having established an improvised hospital in Cambridge Hall. For some, however, these exercises and drills were a little too real.

Some of the street collectors for Alexandra Rose Day 1914.

17

As Europe edged ever closer to war people were under no illusions that it was not a question of if but when there was going to be war with Germany.

In late July the permanent staff of Territorial Infantry Brigades began to set up offices in many key towns, in some cases immediately after their summer camps. The adjutants of the various battalions made arrangements to place themselves in close contact with their respective headquarters and kept a weather eye on the post offices who had extended the hours of their telegraph service in the event of urgent announcements or orders being transmitted. On Thursday 30 July the first precautionary deployments of British military forces on home soil were made. The Special Section of 'A' (Morpeth) Company, 7th Battalion, Northumberland Fusiliers was called out for duty on the coast, the Northern Cyclist's Battalion, at that time still on camp at Bridlington, received orders to immediately mobilise their Special Service Companies too. Twelve hundred soldiers from the Grenadier Guards and Sherwood Foresters were drafted up to Newcastle, Tynemouth, North and South Shields, closely followed by a Company of the East Yorkshire Regiment direct from camp at Conway, Wales and a Royal Navy battle fleet of 30 vessels was sent for the defence of the Tyne.

Over the weekend of 1 and 2 August a palpable military presence manifested in both coastal and urban areas where soldiers were posted to guard key areas such as railway stations, the high level and swing bridges, utilities like the gas works, oil tanks, wireless stations and military installations. Searchlights were also in operation to keep a sharp look out on all incoming vessels at Tynemouth. First Lord of the Admiralty Sir Winston Churchill instigated the full mobilisation of the Fleet and the Admiralty order calling up all classes of naval reserves reached some towns as early as 4.00am on the morning of Sunday 2 August. Newspapers were able to report on 3 August that the Royal Fleet Reserve and Royal Naval Reserve had been called out and preparations completed, that all the effective ships of the Fleet were in a state of instant readiness and every seaman, Marine or Reserve was at his post of duty.

On the world's stage on Monday 3 August the situation was that Germany had requested that Belgium let its troops pass through but Belgium had categorically refused and asked Britain to intervene and request an assurance that Belgian wishes would be respected. The request had been sent and the world watched and waited for the response. Monday 3 August was a Bank Holiday in England and was described in numerous newspapers as 'one of the strangest ever known' because, in the light of the impending national emergency the London and South Western and North Eastern Railway Companies announced the evening before that they had been 'compelled to cancel all excursions.' Many country functions were affected as a result but a large number of Novocastrians determined to spend a day in the country at popular spots like Jesmond Dene or at the seaside and went out of the city aboard horse drawn brakes, in motor cars or aboard a chara-a-banc. Some even ventured on a trip to Whitby aboard the steamer *Earl of Aberdeen* or a sail along the coast in the ferry *G.H. Dexter*.

As the emerging world crisis intensified some events were cancelled and other regular Bank Holiday sporting and social events such as the Police Sports at St. James's Park, Blaydon Races, Morpeth Olympic Games, Tyneside Show at Hexham and the cricket match, Northumberland v. Durham at Chester-le-Street all lacked something of their usual animation and charm. As the *Newcastle Daily Journal* commented: 'For all the sunshine however, there was a cloud of which cognisance could not be lost, which there is little doubt made the holiday for many people, one scarcely to be remembered with gladness – the cloud of war. Wherever people congregated, the conflict on the continent was the chief topic of conversation and one naturally which could not be discussed without anxiety.'

The seaside resorts were densely thronged with visitors who drew up in large numbers along the marine parades and sea fronts to watch the Royal Naval

Reservists and members of the Tyne Division of the Royal Naval Volunteer Reserve muster up and march to report themselves to their appointed centres. The French Consulate offices at 11, Saville Row were also busy throughout the day. France had already introduced conscription and the young French men eligible for military service that were resident in Newcastle had already had forty-eight hours grace to report to the office to get instructions for their call-up.

As the hours passed no reply was received from

Fenham Barracks, Newcastle c.1914.

Germany to the English request. Though the shops, like the factories and shipyards, were closed, the principal streets of Newcastle were unusually thronged. Throughout the day people continuously gathered in front of newspaper offices, and hung around thoroughfares where the latest bulletins were posted. Fluctuations of hope noticeable during the day began to settle at nightfall into a fixed feeling that the worst must be expected and throughout that hot late summer night groups stood about the streets discussing the likely developments of the morrow.

On the world stage, on Tuesday 4 August, Sir Edward Grey, (a descendant of the Earl Grey honoured on the great Newcastle monument) the Secretary of Foreign Affairs wired to the British ambassador in Berlin asking for a reply from Germany before midnight. During the day more soldiers were placed on guard at main post offices in larger towns. There was certainly a martial feeling that pervaded the city and it had direct effects upon the civilian population too. Despite official warnings against hoarding, provision merchants had a massive increase in sales of tinned food and comments were made in the press about how the prices were being inflated and unnecessary shortages being caused. Such concern was felt about these shortages a proclamation was issued on posters and in the newspapers by the Mayor that in the event of chronic shortages depots for the distribution of food would be established in the city. A public appeal for volunteers to man these in the event of such an emergency was made and the Chief Constable was instructed to enrol Special Constables 'as a precautionary measure.'

During the day of 4 August excitement was caused when the posters mobilizing the Army Reserve went up around the city and the majority of the 1,766 Reservists of the Northumberland Fusiliers were soon seen wending their way up Barrack Road to their Depot to be medically inspected and issued with uniforms, equipment, rifles and ammunition. The *Journal* recorded: 'There was no mistaking these Reservists, for all their civilian attire. They had the upright carriage and swinging step that proclaimed the old soldier at once.' Some of them were accompanied by their wives, many of them with young children clinging to their skirts, there was many a moving scene as the women dashed the tears from their eyes as they bade their 'bonny lad' go and do his duty. Within 48 hours all but 44 of the Reservists had reported for duty. Some had come many miles from their new post army lives as far away as Aberdeen and the Isle of Wight and most of those missing were believed to be working on fishing boats and merchant vessels at sea. They were divided by class of Reservist those from the first class were sent direct to the 1st Battalion in Portsmouth, second class went to Territorial units and third class sent for Home Defence.

Throughout the evening of 4 August the crowds had gradually swollen in front of the telegraph and newspaper offices as the ultimatum deadline approached, along the coast as the light faded many lingered on the sea fronts where it was widely recorded 'the lights of warcraft were discernible.' At 11pm the message came that war had been declared against Germany it was greeted with cheers and the streets rang with patriotic songs, the drink flowed, streamers were thrown and flags were waved. It was the last ebullient burst of celebration from an age of innocence in blissful ignorance of the cataclysm that was to come. Nothing would ever be the same again.

Sunday morning on Newcastle Quayside shortly before war broke out in 1914.

Mobilisation

At the time of the outbreak of war the men of 1st Battalion, Northumberland Fusiliers had just returned to their Barracks at Portsmouth after camp at Wool and mobilised with the smooth efficiency that was the hallmark of the professional soldiers of 1914. Joined by a smart body of Reservists they were a very fine looking battalion that marched out on 13 August 1914 to become part of 9th Brigade, 3rd Infantry Division, British Expeditionary Force in France where they landed the following day. The battalion were soon in action at the opening battles of the war at Mons, the Aisne and at the First Battle of Ypres.

Meanwhile, the 2nd Battalion, Northumberland Fusiliers were on the other side of the world stationed at Sabathu, India. They had been in sweltering heat and were grateful to have the monsoon break shortly before war broke out. Returned to England in November 1914 the battalion first arrived on the Western Front in January 1915 but they would be in the fighting lines soon enough at the Second Battle of Ypres and at the Battle of Loos.

The men of Northumberland's Territorial Force Battalions were mobilised and ordered to proceed to their headquarters immediately on the morning of 5 August 1914. There was not a Territorial Corps in Newcastle which had not a good report to make as to numbers and promptness with which their members had assembled. Large crowds gathered from early on to cheer the Reservists and the county companies of the Territorials as they arrived by train to report at their Barracks or Headquarters in Newcastle. Some went straight from their places of work to take up arms while through the night a constant stream of khaki clad figures were seen on the streets in brakes and other vehicles and on bicycles, many of them with family and friends to cheer them along. Many a tear was shed by

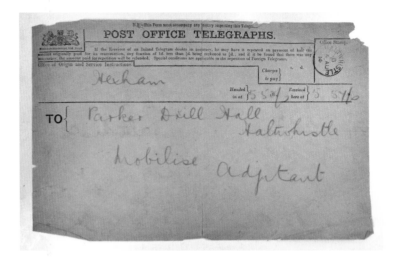

The telegram ordering the mobilisation of the Territorials at Haltwhistle, 4 August 1914 (FMN).

mothers, sisters and wives on that morning as their dear ones parted from them.

The 6th Battalion, Northumberland Fusiliers had been told to parade at 6am, it was, however, impossible for all the men to gather that early but by 7am almost the entire battalion had gathered at St. George's Drill Hall under the command of Lieut.-Col. G. R. B. Spain. Officers and men were medically examined then two companies were ordered to relieve the Regular soldiers on guard at Central Station and other key locations of the city, others were sent to prepare stores and transport and to arrange billets for the battalion. Five companies ended up in Tilley's Rooms on Market Street and one company was sent to Benwell. Indeed, almost every available space in the city appeared to be taken up by Territorials of one corps or another on the night of 5 August, some camped on the Leazes, others at Gosforth, even St Thomas's Churchyard was occupied by men and horses, the animals being seen peacefully grazing there.

There was a big rush of recruits to a number of the Drill Halls, a number of the young men who had walked with their pals to wish them well walked in with them to volunteer and a considerable number of 'useful artisans' signed up for the Territorial Royal Engineers at their headquarters in Barras Bridge. After a number of moves to dig trenches and garrison key areas in Newcastle and along the coast by 30 August all four of the Territorial Battalions of the Northumberland Infantry Brigade were under canvas at Gosforth Park.

Patriotism was high but some concerns were mentioned in the press over the number of men who had been employed on public services such as Newcastle Post Office, the tramways or City Police Force that had left having been called to the Navy or Army Reserve or mobilised as Territorials. That said, a number of employers were keen to show their patriotism too; among the first was the Newcastle and Gateshead Gas Company who gave a public assurance that the wives of married Reservists and Territorials who were required to be absent from their employ would be ensured a weekly allowance and that all those who left to serve would be guaranteed re-employment on their return, a gesture soon echoed by the Newcastle Corporation Tramways and a number of other local businesses.

Territorial Force soldiers were not obliged to serve overseas, their job was to defend the home territory but it soon became apparent there could well be a need for the men of the Territorial Force to serve in theatres of war abroad. The question was asked if they were willing to sign up for active service and the response was that eighty per cent of them agreed, they were designated Imperial Service Battalions and the men who had volunteered were soon issued with 'Imperial Service' badges which they wore with pride just above the right breast pocket of their jacket.

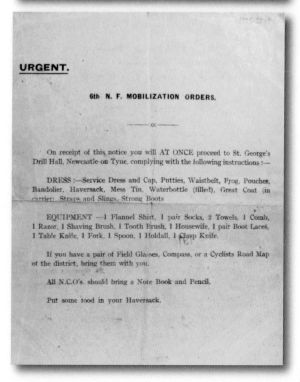

The mobilisation notice sent to Pte. J. Walden of 6th (Newcastle) Battalion, Northumberland Fusiliers (T.F.) advising him to report to St. George's Drill Hall for 6am on 5 August 1914 (FMN)..

Clockwise from top left: 1) Multi-view postcard showing the 188th Brigade, Northumberland Fusiliers (T.F.) while at training camp 1915. 2) A patriotic postcard for the Northumberland Fusiliers 1914. 3) A young Northumberland Fusilier Territorial soldier proudly wearing his Imperial Service badge. 4) An Imperial Service badge, presented to all Territorial Force soldiers that volunteered to serve overseas before 30 September 1914. 5) Men of the 6th Battalion, Northumberland Fusiliers (T.F.) outside St. George's Drill Hall, Newcastle, 1914.

Departure of the 6th Battalion,
Northumberland Fusiliers (T.F.)
from Seaton Sluice, for France
April 1915.

‘YOU ARE THE MAN I WANT’

Your King and Country Need You.

A CALL TO ARMS.

An addition of 100,000 men to his Majesty's Regular Army is immediately necessary in the present grave National Emergency.

Lord Kitchener is confident that this appeal will be at once responded to by all those who have the safety of our Empire at heart.

TERMS OF SERVICE.

General Service for a period of 3 years or until the war is concluded.

Age of Enlistment between 19 and 30.

HOW TO JOIN.

Full information can be obtained at any Post Office in the Kingdom or at any Military depot.

GOD SAVE THE KING!

Left: The iconic image of Lord Kitchener and his pointing finger calling you to join Kitchener's Army in 1914.

Above: The original 'Your King and Country Need You' poster appealing for volunteers for Kitchener's Army published in August 1914.

Kitchener's Army

When England sends her banner forth,
And bids her armour shine,
She'll not forget the famous North,
The lads of moor and Tyne.

from *The Old and Bold* by Henry Newbolt (1862-1938)

On the 5 August 1914, the day after Britain had declared war on Germany, Liberal government leader Herbert Asquith announced that Field Marshal Horatio Herbert Kitchener had been made Secretary of State for War. Kitchener, or 'K of K' (Kitchener of Khartoum) as he was often known, was a national hero whose name was synonymous with military achievement and victories and whose appointment inspired confidence in the British people at this critical time.

He had come to prominence during the colonial wars of the second half of the nineteenth century. The Egyptian campaigns of the mid-1880s furthered his reputation during the re-conquest of the Sudan culminating in victory at the Battle of Omdurman in 1898 and again against the Boers during the Anglo-Boer War 1899-1902. The Field Marshal was an illustrator's dream, looking every inch the epitome of the senior British Army officer his apparently imperturbable and sternly martial features regularly appeared in newspapers and magazines and on all manner of patriotic souvenirs from Sunday school prize books and certificates to decorative plates and tea caddies.

Beyond the hype Kitchener personally abhorred red tape and had no tolerance for any interference or opposition; he hated delegation and worked tirelessly to see things through. This did not always make him popular with the War Office but it meant he was without doubt the best man for the job at that moment in time. Kitchener was one of few senior British officers far-sighted enough to see that a major European war was not going to be over by Christmas and he was of the opinion that the country should prepare itself for a three year period in which some seventy divisions would be required. To have sufficient numbers of trained soldiers to fight for Britain, a country in which conscription would not be introduced until January 1916, he would have to step up recruitment. Kitchener believed that the existing military organisation of the British army was wholly inadequate, he had been opposed to the creation of what he termed the 'unwieldy' Territorial Force in 1908 and was not prepared to expand the Territorials to fill the manpower gap. He wanted a New Army of volunteer soldiers who would be proud to say that they were 'Kitchener's men.' In Cabinet, Kitchener was second only to the Prime Minister, Cabinet members were intimidated by his reputation and dared not question him over his decisions where matters of directing the war were concerned so when he pressed for the expansion of the Army by 500,000 it was sanctioned the same day and announcements that recruitment for the first 100,000 volunteers would begin on 11 August 1914 appeared in the press soon afterwards. Local newspapers published lists of the places where the men could enlist. In Newcastle it was the Infantry Barracks and the National Service League Offices, Saville Chambers, Saville Row and the Territorial Force Drill Halls around the county at Alnwick, Amble, Ashington, Blyth, Haltwhistle, Hexham, Morpeth, Newburn, Wooler and North Shields followed by Prudhoe and Wallsend on 14 August, such were the numbers of men wanting to join up.

Kitchener's famous call to arms, 'Your King and

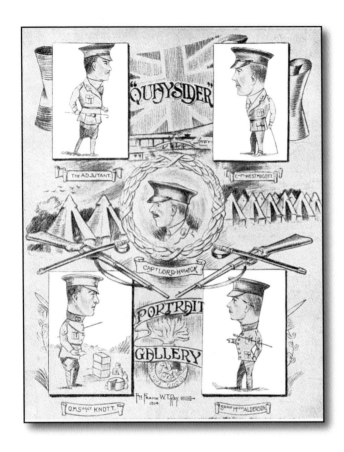

One of a number of fine illustrations drawn in 1914 by Pte. Frank Ray of B Company, 9th Battalion, Northumberland Fusiliers known as the 'Quaysiders' after the area of Newcastle they were predominantly recruited from.

Country Need You', called for men between the ages of nineteen and thirty to enlist although former soldiers were accepted up to the age of forty-five.

The pressure was on the men of Britain to answer that call. The British Empire was a force to be reckoned with and worth fighting for, while the generation targeted by Kitchener had been educated to possess a sense of duty and obligation to both King and country. The iconic image of Kitchener, with his pointing finger and hypnotic eyes appeared everywhere on magazines, posters and even postcards. Alongside the Kitchener poster there were many others calling for men to 'Join our Happy Throng' to help defend Britain and all it stood for from 'the marauding Huns'. Some posters ignored the appeal to patriotism and instead questioned any man's motives for not joining up. One quoted Lord Kitchener, asking men to 'be certain that your so called reason is not a selfish excuse', while young women were asked to consider 'Why is your boy not in khaki?' Such appeals saw groups of young girls arm themselves with white feathers, which could be presented on the street or sent through the post to any man not thought to be 'doing his bit'.

Within two weeks Kitchener had his first 100,000 recruits and what became known as 'K1,' the first six divisions of the New Army were approved by the War Office and a further four New Armies would be formed under the Kitchener scheme by the end of 1914.

Recruiting for the 8th (Service) Battalion, Northumberland Fusiliers was truly magnificent, some 1,100 men were enlisted in the first eleven days and this battalion has the distinction of being recognised as the very first complete battalion of any English Regiment in Kitchener's Army (Registered complete 21 August 1914).

Such were the numbers of volunteers for the

battalion those surplus to the establishment were sent to York to join another Service Battalion whose numbers had not been filled at so rapid a rate. This decision was not a popular one and further Service battalions for the Northumberland Fusiliers were soon sanctioned. There was never a problem with recruitment in Newcastle or the county for the seven pre-war battalions of The Northumberland Fusiliers. These expanded during the course of the war to a staggering fifty-two battalions, twenty-nine of which served overseas. This made them the second largest regiment in the British Army, with only the eighty-eight battalions of the London Regiment surpassing them in greater number.

After initially being accommodated in a variety of school buildings in Newcastle and experiencing a number of depravations suffered by many of the battalions raised so quickly such as a lack of uniforms, food taking forty minutes to serve due to logistics and shortages of plates and utensils, the 8th Battalion departed for its first training camp at Belton Park, Grantham, Lincolnshire on 27 August 1914.

As the appeal went out for Kitchener's 'Second Hundred Thousand' recruiting drives were held in towns and villages across the country. There were public meetings led by local dignitaries with the clergy and military officers delivering speeches voicing 'appeals to patriotism', a fleet of decorated motor cars carrying dignitaries, soldiers, veterans, drummers

and pipers toured Newcastle and district and military bands filled marketplaces with music to draw the crowds for the speakers and flags and bunting aplenty flapped in the breeze. In Newcastle local ship owner Sir George Renwick M.P. was prominent in the recruitment scheme and all five of his own sons would serve in the war. In late August Earl Grey conveyed Kitchener's direct appeal to the Northumberland Miners, speaking to large gatherings of the men from Bedlington, Seaton Delaval, Broomhill and Amble stating Kitchener had told him directly:

'Tell them from me that I have often had occasion to thank Heaven that I had the Northumberland Fusiliers at my back. Tell them from me that I have often relied upon the Northumberland Fusiliers in the past and I know that I may need to do so in the future. I need their assistance and those who give me their aid will have an opportunity of proving their worth.'

Some new recruits for a Northumberland Fusiliers Service Battalion, 1914. Note some of the men have uniform jacket and trousers but are still wearing their flat caps.

"The Lads of Halton Park."

By a Private in the 13th Northumberland Fusiliers now stationed at Halton.

OF all the acres the Rothschilds own,
  And there are many neat and smart,
The one that is distinguished most
  Is christened Halton Park.

Over five and twenty thousand
  Bold recruits have made a start
To train to fight the Germans
  In this glorious Halton Park.

Up early in the morning
  They go singing like the lark,
To get their steaming cocoa
  From the cook-house in the Park.

Then the sight at night is splended,
  Especially after dark,
When the tents are lit with candles
  In this spacious Halton Park.

And when they're trained and ready
  For the front, and they embark,
You will hear the people shout
  "There's the lad's from Halton Park."

Then, when Berlin is taken,
  The Kaiser will remark
"Where do those demons come from?"
  The answer—"Halton Park."

When our arms have been victorious,
  And each man has made his mark:
Where will the highest honour go?
  Why, to the lads of Halton Park.

[*Reprinted from the "Buck's Herald" of Nov. 14, 1914.*]

Clockwise from top left: 1) 'Kitchener Volunteers' for 14th (Service) Battalion, Northumberland Fusiliers at Halton Park Camp, Buckinghamshire 1914 (BE). 2) A cheery rhyme written by a soldier of 13th (Service) Battalion, Northumberland Fusiliers while in training camp at Halton Park, November 1914. 3) Officers and men of the 14th (Service) Battalion, Northumberland Fusiliers 1914. Note some of the men have been made NCOs and wear their stripes on their civilian suits (BE).

As Grey read the statement it was greeted by cheers and the newspapers were able to quote impressive numbers of local men coming forward to volunteer every day.

From the outbreak of war, recruitment of volunteers was a phenomena that saw private individuals, school old boys, businesses and groups of friends from a particular area of a town or city banding together to go and join up so they could train and serve together. In many areas of the North they became known as 'Pals' Battalions. Although there were no battalions that bore that nick-name in Northumberland the bonds were just as strong in units that were raised such as The Newcastle Commercials, Tyneside Scottish and the Tyneside Irish.

The first of their kind in our area came out of the efforts of the Newcastle and Gateshead Chamber of Commerce and they became known as 'The Quaysiders.' On 28 August, the very day after the men of the 8th (Service) Battalion left Newcastle, it was announced the War Office had granted permission for the Chamber of Commerce to raise a company of 250 men. The quota was reached in a handful of days, many of the volunteers came from the offices, shops and businesses of the Quayside hence these lads became known as and were very proud to be called 'Quaysiders.' Not least because of a large party of young men from Parson's Works at Heaton who all marched together under a banner bearing the name of their works to jon up a few days later. What they lacked in military training they made up for in enthusiasm and in a few days they were given orders to proceed to their training camp outside Newcastle as the new B Company of 9th (Service) Battalion, Northumberland Fusiliers. How true their company song would prove to be:

'Just a Company of penmen-
Soldiers then, of little worth;
But we set the ball a-rolling
In the hard and fighting North.'

Recruiting had been such in the county that both the 9th and 10th (Service) Battalions, left Newcastle together in four trains bound for the 1st Battalion's recent stomping ground of Bovington Camp, Wool, Dorsetshire on 7 September. After fourteen hours on the train the battalions arrived to find there were no tents and a dearth of blankets and had to content themselves sleeping in the open. Fortunately the Depot Quartermaster had ensured they had plenty of rations to hand on their arrival and by sticking it out they gave the locals an idea of what our 'canny north-country men' were made of.

As August rolled into September an average 33,000 recruits were enlisting nationally on a daily basis and more battalions were being formed all the time. The 11th (Service) Battalion marched to the Central Station on 17 September bound for Bullswater Camp, Pirbright, Surrey where they were joined by the 10th (Service) Battalion along with the 13th and 14th (Service) Battalions of the Durham Light Infantry to form 68 Brigade of the 23rd Division (Part of 'K3'). The problem was however, that after hours on the train then marching the three miles or so to camp they found that the contractor in charge of supplies had only been warned to provide meals for two thousand men not the four thousand that had arrived there.

It was also on 17 September that the first officer and 991 N.C.Os and men of 12th (Service) Battalion travelled down from Newcastle to Aylesbury and over the next few days the rest of the battalion followed to their new camp at Halton Park, Tring, Hertfordshire and it was while they were there, on Sunday 25 September, that the Brigade was inspected personally during a visit by the Secretary of State for War, Lord Kitchener who expressed himself 'completely satisfied' with the appearance of the Brigade, despite the fact that many were still in their civilian shirt sleeves, waistcoats and caps.

The new 14th (Service) Battalion were also sent to Halton Park and their plaintive cry published in the regimental journal, The *St George's Gazette* echoed the feeling of every other New Army Battalion of the Northumberland Fusiliers at that time:

'It will be noticed that we are very short of senior officers and if this should meet the eye of any old Fifth man just returned from Timbuctoo or Patagonia, who has not yet made his choice, he will know where he will be made welcome.'

The 13th and the 14th (Service) Battalions became part of the 62nd Infantry Brigade, 21st Division of the Third New Army ('K3'). The 15th (Service) Battalion was formed at Darlington in October 1914 and assigned to 89th Brigade, 30th Division of the Fourth New Army ('K4'). However, 'K4' was not completely formed when a decision was made to turn the 15th and others into Reserve Battalions to provide reinforcements for the three earlier New Armies and the Division was finally broken up in April 1915.

Although there had been moves to raise a Newcastle battalion in the first days after the outbreak of war it was nearly a month later on 2 September 1914, at a meeting of the Council of the Newmarket and Gateshead Chamber of Commerce that Sir George Renwick M.P. proposed the Chamber should ask the Lord Mayor to raise a battalion for the Northumberland Fusiliers from among the citizens of Newcastle. On 8 September 1914 the War Office accepted the offer of a battalion to be raised by the Chamber, the call to 'young commercial men' emblazoned on red-lettered posters went up across the city and Recruiting Offices were opened at 91, Grey Street and 33, Sandhill in Newcastle with two more, one at 15, High Street, Gateshead and at 42, Howard Street, North Shields.

The battalion was completed in less than a week then registered and acknowledged by the War Office as such on 16 September 1914. Thus began the first Battalion of the New Army to be completely raised by civilian effort in Newcastle and is claimed to have been the first of its kind in the North. A 'Pals' battalion in all but name, they became known as the 'Newcastle Commercials,' and had their first drill sessions on the Royal Grammar School field where they were soon issued with their first uniform – a red cord around the right shoulder to signify the wearer had answered the call of his King and country.

Meanwhile, on the North Eastern Railway over two thousand men had already left to join the army and the navy. When the Army Council was looking for further assistance in raising men the management took up the mantle to give other railwaymen the chance of serving with their friends and colleagues in a North Eastern Railway Battalion. Given formal sanction on 11 September, recruiting began on 14 September at York and Newcastle and the new battalion grew rapidly. At the time there were already around 7,000 recruits in Newcastle causing a major shortage of billets, a situation repeated in many other cities and major towns. Consequently the volunteers of the North Eastern Railway were all despatched to Hull where the battalion was officially raised at the King George Dock. The Dock was the joint property of the North Eastern

Railway and the Hull and Barnsley Railway Companies, the latter of which kindly allowed two of their warehouses to be converted to barracks and by 1 October 1914 the whole battalion was assembled there and officially known as 17th (Service) Battalion, Northumberland Fusiliers (N.E.R. Pioneers).

Newcastle had certainly not seen the raising of its last battalion. The success of the recruitment of the Commercials saw the military committee of Newcastle and Gateshead Chamber of Trade press to raise more battalions. On 10 October Lord Chancellor Haldane, the man who as War Minister had created the modern British army, paid an official visit to Newcastle. He inspected the Commercials on the Grammar School field and at patriotic meetings before huge audiences at the Tyne and Pavilion Theatres he announced three more battalions were wanted – Scottish, Irish and a second Commercial Battalion.

The Chamber received permission to raise its next battalion on 14 October and at 2pm on 16 October the first thirty or forty volunteers, all of whom had enlisted and taken the oath, gathered on the County Cricket Ground to fall in for their first session of drill. They were also issued their first kit from the pavilion – rather like the Commercials with their red cord – each recruit was given a piece of yellow window cord to be sewn onto the right shoulder of his jacket to signify he had now joined the unit known as the 'Second Commercials.' They wore that cord with quite some pride but one recruit was somewhat annoyed when he overheard one passer-by on Grainger Street explain to another that he understood the cord to mean 'Yes, he's tried to enlist, but has been marked medically unfit.' When completed in November 1914 the 'Second Commercials' were adopted as 18th (Service) Battalion, Northumberland Fusiliers and marched off on 21

December to the Central station from a snow covered Cricket Ground bound for their new camp at Rothbury.

With the success of yet another Commercials battalion there were hopes of providing a Newcastle Brigade (four battalions serving together) including an Old Boy Scout's Company but the dream was not to be, the War Office granted permission for the Newcastle and Gateshead Chamber of Commerce to raise what proved to be its last battalion on 14 November 1914. The Third Newcastle Commercials rapidly received 650 names for its ranks and the first call to them, from Major Temperley, was published on 16 November whereby

'All men who have registered their names and can shoot with a rifle are requested to report themselves at the recruiting office, 91, Grey Street, as early as possible today.'

The Battalion rapidly took shape, there were over 800 men on parade by late November and they soon picked up an added pride as they marched out with a fine set of drums and fifes presented by Mr. Frederick George Storey proprietor of the *Newcastle Journal*. The Third Tyneside Commercials were soon completed and formally titled 19th (Service) Battalion, Northumberland Fusiliers. After having their headquarters at 20, Osborne Avenue in Jesmond, they moved to camp at Morpeth in early 1915 and it was later, in the February that same year both the 18th and 19th Battalions were designated Pioneer battalions (1st and 2nd Tyneside Pioneers respectively).

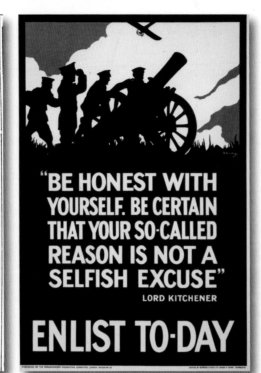

THE NEWCASTLE AND TYNESIDE

COMMERCIAL BATTALIONS,

Now the 16th, 18th, & 19th (Service) Battns. Northumberland Fusiliers.

The above Battalions have each been called upon to raise a

Depot Company of 250 Men.

These have been partly filled up, but there is still an opportunity for about 400 Men to be associated with the

3,700 Commercials of Newcastle & Tyneside

who have already enlisted.

Those who wish to join their friends in serving their King and Country should ENLIST AT ONCE, so that the Training of all the Men of the Depot Companies may proceed simultaneously.

JOIN AT ONCE.

Recruiting Offices :—

91, Grey Street, Newcastle-on-Tyne.
33, Sandhill, Newcastle-on-Tyne.
15, High Street, Gateshead.
42, Howard Street, North Shields.

"BE HONEST WITH YOURSELF. BE CERTAIN THAT YOUR SO-CALLED REASON IS NOT A SELFISH EXCUSE"

LORD KITCHENER

ENLIST TO-DAY

G. R.

THE NEW ARMIES

More Men are Needed at once

COMPLETE THE SECOND HALF-MILLION

and ensure

SUCCESS ABROAD AND SAFETY AT HOME

ENLIST FOR THE PERIOD OF THE WAR

Arrangements are now complete to receive and train all who enlist.

STANDARDS HAVE BEEN LOWERED

Apply at any Military Barrack or Recruiting Office; the addresses of the latter can be obtained from Post Offices or Labour Exchanges.

War Office, 19th October, 1914.

GOD SAVE THE KING.

THERE IS STILL A PLACE IN THE LINE FOR YOU

THIS SPACE IS RESERVED FOR A FIT MAN

Will you fill it?

IF THE CAP FITS YOU

JOIN THE ARMY TO-DAY.

Clockwise from top left: 1) Newspaper advert recruiting to the Newcastle and Tyneside Commercial Battalions, 1914. 2) A poster issuing a reminder from Lord Kitchener for men to reconsider if their reason for not joining the army is actually a 'selfish excuse' 1914. 3) An appeal to complete the second half million volunteers issued in October 1914. 4) One of the many posters for the ongoing recruitment campaign for men to join up. 5) One of the popular recruiting posters often seen on railway stations and at recruiting rallies around the country.

Recruiting and Recruits

The Kitchener campaign was a remarkable success but as the battalions marched away to war and more and more battalions were raised, it soon became apparent that a significant number of men who would have made good soldiers had been turned away from recruiting offices for the sake of a few inches in height so the requisite height was lowered and the age limit was raised, but for some even with these adjustments they still didn't quite meet the official recruitment criteria. However some men were not above bending the rules so that they too could 'do their bit.'

Both middle-aged and young men adjusted their ages in order to enlist. A tale familiar in most parts of the country tells of young, well-built lads presenting themselves to recruiting sergeants, admitting to be sixteen years old (but would pass for nineteen), and being told to 'go out, then come back in and tell me different'. Put right by soldiers outside the lad would go back in, lie about his age and off he went to war. In a similar vein, if one medical officer found you unfit for military service another recruiting office under pressure to up their numbers after the initial burst of volunteers may have a different opinion.

In *The First Day on the Somme* by Martin Middlebrook, Pte. B. Richardson of the Newcastle Commercials would recall: 'I tried to enlist but, after waiting two hours with crowds of others, I was examined by a doctor and was rejected. My chest only measured twenty-eight inches. I went across the Tyne on the ferry and tried the recruiting office at North Shields. I found the doctor there more easily suited and he marked my chest as thirty-eight inches. I went home and told my mother but she cried, saying I was only a boy. I was eighteen!'

The response of the Newcastle men to their country's call was truly outstanding, battalion after battalion was raised and the newspapers reeled out stories and rows of photographs showing the uniformed portraits of families with three, four and even five sons that had all 'answered their country's call.'

Schools, churches, chapels, sports clubs and societies collated the names of their old boys and members into rolls that were published or displayed honouring all those who had volunteered to do their bit. Mr. E. Dougherty, the headmaster of St. Mary's Roman Catholic Boy's School on Bath Lane Terrace, Newcastle prepared a list of 'Old Boys' who were serving with the colours, by 30 October 1914 there were 443 on the list.

Professional footballers from Newcastle Town F.C. were among the first to join the 'Newcastle Commercials' and even amateur clubs did their bit such as Cramlington Villa that contributed five of their players and even members of their management committee to Kitchener's Army in 1914. All the Newcastle Battalions had keen and competitive football teams while in training and even when they went overseas.

Men from all walks of life volunteered to become Kitchener men, there were the 'white collar' clerks, shop workers, tram drivers, railway workers and even stars of music hall like the well-known ventriloquist Arthur Prince who closed his contract at the Newcastle Hippodrome to join the 'Commercials.'

Miners and shipyard workers answered the call by the thousand, by 11 November 1914 Heworth Colliery alone had supplied 470 men for the Colours but such

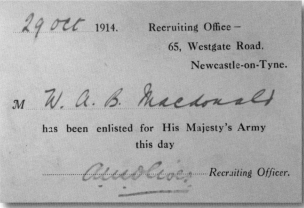

Clockwise from top left: 1) A German propaganda card for the sinking of the Hogue, Cressy and Aboukir by the U.9 on 22 September 1914. 2) Local people were particularly incensed by the shelling of Hartlepool where eighty-six civilians and seven soldiers were killed. A further 424 civilians and seven soldiers were injured in the attack.3) One of the cards given to lads by Newcastle Recruiting Officers to prove they had enlisted (FMN).

were the numbers leaving to 'do their bit' concerns were expressed over maintaining production and there was a ban on miners enlisting until they could stabilise numbers working in the collieries. Although there were peaks and troughs in the flow of men coming forward each new appeal was answered with renewed enthusiasm. Because of this the continued existence of women and girls presenting men on the street with white feathers in October 1914 caused Newcastle's Lord Mayor to publicly state he was 'ashamed of those ladies' because there was 'no need to distribute white feathers amongst the young men of Tyneside.'

Recruits from a number of locations around the British Empire could be found in the ranks of the Northumberland Fusiliers in 1914. Some of the sons of Newcastle who had emigrated to our Colonies or Dominions returned to the county of their birth to join up in their local Regiment. Others were from distant shores like James Jeffries, born in Bombay to a British father and an Indian mother. Living in Britain for the previous six years he chose to join the 2nd Battalion, Tyneside Irish. A number of lads of mixed race from Newcastle were also in the ranks and were affectionately known as 'Smoked Geordies.' There was even Eldridge Eastman, a black Canadian and professional sprinter who was in New Brunswick when war broke out and was blighted in his attempts to join up because black and Japanese Canadians were not allowed to enlist in Canadian forces at that time so he travelled to Britain and joined the Northumberland Fusiliers.

In November 1914, it was calculated the net result of the recruitment campaign was that 20,000 had been attested in Newcastle for Kitchener's Army, concurrently there had also been successful recruiting for the Royal Naval Volunteer Reserve, Hussars, Corps and even the Royal Flying Corps.

So why was the Kitchener campaign so successful? For modern generations it is hard to get our minds around patriotism but for the boys raised in the ethos of 'doing their bit' for King and Country it really was the right thing to do. There were voices of dissent on pacifist and religious grounds but they really were in the minority.

Anglo-German political and military relations had not been good for the majority of the ten years before the First World War and fears and mistrust of the German nation had been compounded in popular literature such as *Riddle of the Sands* (1903) by Erskine Childers, William le Queux's *The Invasion of 1910* (1906) and *Spies of the Kaiser* (1909). The latter being a book with such loaded chapter titles as 'The Peril of England,' 'The Back Door of England' and 'How the Germans are Preparing for Invasion' ably demonstrates the tenor of such literature which reached its zenith in the early years of the war with John Buchan's *Thirty-Nine Steps* (1915). When war broke out anti-German acts of vandalism and even instances of riot occurred. Newspapers carried notices of how and why 'enemy aliens' had to be identified and an atmosphere of spy-mania erupted, fuelled by both old fears and reportage in both national and local newspapers of the 'German Desperadoes in England'. These stories claiming to be based on some foreign intelligence alleged some of them had been among us for some years and each one of them was on a mission bent on destruction of the infrastructure, transport network and utilities of Britain; hence the posting of troops on the likes of the railways, key bridges and gas works from the eve of war.

Recruitment was further stimulated by the outrage many people felt as more stories reached Britain of 'the rape of Belgium' by German forces. It was also mooted that the opening battles of the war could have been won if they had only had more men. Then on Tuesday 22 September 1914 the Royal Navy armoured Cruisers *Aboukir, Hogue* and *Cressy*, then engaged keeping North Sea waters south of Dogger Bank clear of German torpedo craft and mine layers, were all sunk by the German submarine U.9 under the Command of Kapitänleutnant Otto Weddigen. A significant number of the Royal Naval Reserve men who had been given such a send-off from the Tyne at the opening of the war had been posted to those vessels and distressing scenes were witnessed along the river and coast as the Admiralty announced the losses.

Recruitment was fuelled yet again after ships came from the 1st and 2nd Scouting Group of the Imperial German Navy under the command of Konteradmiral Franz von Hipper and shelled the British coast at Scarborough, Whitby and Hartlepool on 16 December 1914 resulting in 137 fatalities and almost 600 injured. The press response was clear, under the banner of 'Tynesiders asked to Avenge German Raid,' the *Illustrated Chronicle* quoted a new recruiting poster at length:

'The wholesale murder of innocent women and children demands vengeance. Men of England, the innocent victims of German brutality call upon you to avenge them. Show the German barbarians that Britain's shores cannot be bombarded with impunity. Duty calls you now. Go to-day to the nearest recruiting depot and offer your services for your King, home and country.'

When all is said and done though, at the most basic level by 1914, in the days before television and mass media, the previous experiences of soldiers in action were distant and coloured by the widely promoted images of victorious British soldiers on campaigns to win the British Empire; joining up was done in quite some naivety as the consequences and carnage of modern warfare were simply not known nor could they have really been predicted in 1914. Most of those who survived to look back in old age on those early months of war in 1914 would consider them some of the greatest times of their life and that they had answered their country's call and joined with their pals with a sense of anticipation in being part of something very special, indeed embarking on the greatest adventure of their lives. They would say with some pride 'I would not have missed it for the world.'

Men of the 12th (Service) Battalion, Northumberland Fusiliers wearing their 'Kitchener Blue' uniforms.

Training Kitchener's Army

The first problem to confront the men of Kitchener's Army was one of accommodation. Recruiting thousands of men, in addition to the mobilized Territorials and new volunteers for the Regular army, meant that billets in extant buildings soon became scarce in the cities and towns where there were barracks and Territorial headquarters. Temporary accommodation was found in all manner of buildings from guest houses to maltings, warehouses to schools, public halls and church rooms while the men were put through their early paces of training on places like the Town Moor, the Royal Grammar School Field or the Country Cricket Ground. Route marches of new volunteer soldiers in training wearing their civilian clothes were common sights around the streets of Newcastle and Jesmond. Coming to grips with drill, however, was not always as easy as it may have appeared, as recalled in the early days of training for the Newcastle Commercials:

'Platoons were formed and Companies began to shape. To accommodate Headquarters, a commodious wooden hut was rapidly erected at the top of the field. Here the stream of recruits was quickly handled by Colonel Ritson and his staff. No finer parade ground could have been obtained than that at the Royal Grammar School. Spacious, yes: and comparatively private. No one was over keen to let a curious public – things military were still objects of curiosity in those early days – see his first endeavours to "jump to it." Feet were not so nimble as they might have been; and, anyway, forming fours was not, at first, so simple as it looked. Instructors, too, and aspiring N.C.O.'s were not so sure of their commands. Was it not a cause for gratitude for extensive grounds when your squad was marching headlong into another squad and you had forgotten the correct command to stay their disastrous course? Praise be to the Grammar School grounds for their size, and even for their privacy in those early days of learning.'

And skills such as previous experience of leadership, perhaps in the Boy's Brigade or Boy Scouts or the ability to fire a rifle set men apart and gave them a good chance of promotion:

'...there was a sudden mysterious call for men with any previous experience of musketry. Imagination took rein; and anyone with even a nodding acquaintance with a man who once saw a gun license believed himself to possess the necessary qualifications. So, too, the expert who had once caused the extinction of a celluloid ball at the "Hoppings" adopted the airs of a Bisley crack.'

From Cooke, Capt. C. H. *Historical Records of the 16th (Service) Battalion Northumberland Fusiliers* (Newcastle 1923)

The accommodation crisis in Newcastle meant these arrangements could not be permanent and to begin fostering regimental *esprit de corps*, many of the freshly raised battalions were soon marched off and sent by the train load to training camps in other parts of the country, in the case of the Northumberland Fusiliers Service Battalions to places such as Bovington, Dorsetshire, Halton in Hertfordshire and Pirbright in Surrey. These camps presented their own problems as there was frequently limited space and up to sixteen men were sleeping in just one bell tent. There were only limited amounts of plates, cups and cutlery so men frequently had to share and appeals were sent back to the home county to provide warm blankets and clothing because the weather was not always good with some camps becoming a sea of mud where the soldiers regularly marched or walked. Fortunately, by the winter of 1914, most of the battalions were at least in wooden barrack huts with coal and wood stoves.

Once at their camps the battalions really began to take shape, training and working together as units. Physical fitness training, route marches and drill continued and additionally, as Pte. Tom Easton recalled of his time at Alnwick Camp:

'Specialist training was now embarked upon. Machine gunners, transport, signallers, runners and all other special links were formed up and the personnel got under training. Guard duties were put on their proper footing and discipline on the whole was greatly intensified. Feeding arrangements were on more collective lines under our own army cooks, which also meant that the troops had to do most of the cookhouse fatigues – including peeling potatoes. Gradually, the whole camp settled down to a military existence and before many weeks were past, it could be said we had so adapted ourselves to the great change that we differed little to any great body of trained troops for the weeding out process was carried out and those unfit were sent elsewhere. Brigade headquarters then took a hand and we were put on the moors up above the town to carry out sham battles under the Brigadier General. During these manoeuvres we were set to digging trenches, afterwards filling them in by way of a bit more practice.'

The question of uniform remained a lingering problem. Officers were more fortunate when it came to clothing and equipment because they bought their own and there were national companies such as the Army & Navy Stores that had bolts of serge, barathea and similar cloth of high quality in various shades of khaki and green and plenty of local tailors to supply the needs of newly-enlisted subalterns.

The 'other ranks' of the Northumberland Fusiliers Kitchener Battalions had to rely on their uniforms, kit

ALNWICK CAMP.

and equipment being issued to them, however, due to acute shortages they had started their training in their own civilian work clothes and boots. Their only military insignia being a coloured cord sewn round the right shoulder. N.C.O ranks were denoted by a piece of ribbon tied around the right arm, red for a sergeant or white for a corporal. If stripes arrived before uniforms were issued they would be sewn onto the civilian jacket of the man appointed to that rank.

Every battalion was keen to get into khaki army uniforms as soon as possible but every one of them was to be frustrated because the supply of khaki material soon ran out. The problem, in fact, was not was not the material but rather the dye. The greatest supplier of material dye before the war was Germany and the supplies in Britain were soon exhausted so we had to increase production of our own dyes. In the meantime some uniform had to be found to fill the gap and for many men it was to be the 'Kitchener Blue'. The jackets and trousers were sourced from uniform stocks held for postmen, prison warders and prisoners, although the uniforms for prisoners tended to be grey and therefore had to be dyed dark navy for Army use! This motley collection of uniform was then crowned with a navy side cap of simple construction. The men of the Service Battalions raised by the Chamber of Commerce (B Company 9th Battalion, 16th, 18th and 19th Battalions) had the backing of the Chamber's Military Committee who offered to buy their khaki uniforms for them, but again to no avail, there simply were not the supplies available. They too had to improvise so a uniform similar to the Kitchener Blue but of more a dull, bluish-grey colour was duly ordered from Messrs Bainbridge & Co.

Captain C. Cooke recorded in the Newcastle Commercials battalion history:

'No one liked the grey uniform. The material was very serviceable and stood much hard wear. But it seemed as though a substitute for khaki meant a relegation to a backwater of military activity. The war would soon be

ALNWICK CAMP.

Far left: Recruits undergoing physical training at Alnwick Camp during the winter of 1914-15. *Middle:* Manoeuvres and training across the pastures near Alnwick Castle 1915. *Left:* Guardroom and huts of the 'Newcastle Commercials' at Alnwick Camp 1915 (FMN).

41

over – and here was the battalion not in khaki. Little did we dream then of what "the duration" was actually to be. Many khaki uniforms were worn out in the dread interval. But the grey it had to be; and every man got a stock size which fitted as it hung. Wonderful sights presented themselves to mockery, only the efforts of their own tailors could bring some of the wearers almost back to their well-garbed selves. Almost, but not quite; for many could never be reconciled to the shortness of the jackets. They felt positively indecent.'

The public didn't know what to make of the strange blue uniforms. Some thought that prison warders had been conscripted to maintain public order; others decided that those wearing blue must be Belgian soldiers, and therefore refugees. For the men of the 18th Battalion, their first issue of military clothing took the form of a grey cap and nothing else, which the men were reluctant to wear with their civilian clothes as the wearer was liable to be mistaken for a tram conductor.

By late 1914, the khaki uniforms were beginning to filter back out but the supply was piecemeal. The history of the 19th (Service) Battalion, Northumberland Fusiliers records the days uniforms arrived when they were still at Jesmond:

'Lieut and Quartermaster H. Perry began to issue uniforms or parts thereof and the long company parades in Osborne Avenue and Holly Avenue were a sight never to be forgotten. Men with putty encased legs sported bowler hats; others had no outward and visible signs of the army except a cap, S. D. with or without badge. The civilian variety of clothes with the odd splashes of khaki rendered the parades picturesque at least.'

Even when khaki uniforms became more plentiful there were still not enough regimental badges to go round and men were left with collar badges or shoulder titles instead of cap badges for a while. Quartermasters were often seen scratching their heads over the delivery of odd items of uniform. There might be jackets for three men, caps for five, puttees for nine and assorted items of leather equipment, such as a crate of fifty ammunition pouches but no belts or cross-straps for them.

The Army looked to its stores and found that its only stockpiles left of personal equipment for other ranks

Using the latest techniques to keep fit, this was the 'war dance' of the 'Commercials' in October 1914.

consisted of pre-1900 pattern whitened hide pouches, belts and cross straps. Unfortunately, Kitchener's men did not have the pipeclay to re-whiten this old equipment and smarten it up, not that there was sufficient equipment to make enough full sets to go round. Most men ended up wearing a belt and one ammunition pouch. Victorian webbing was accompanied by the issue of rifles such as the Long Lee or Lee Metford rifles of similar vintage.

A new type of all leather equipment made simply in leather with brass fittings was brought in as an emergency measure before the end of 1914 and many men went abroad and into action still wearing that same leather equipment. They all knew that their time to go abroad for active service was coming when they were handed the new SMLE rifle.

With typical good humour, Kitchener's men sang a song about their tribulations, featuring Fred Karno, the then 'King of the Comedians' whose company had played the Newcastle Empire shortly before the outbreak of war:

'We are Fred Karno's Army,
The rag-time infantry,
We cannot fight, we cannot shoot,
What God damn use are we?
But when we get to Berlin,
The Kaiser he will say,
Hoch, Hoch, Mein Gott!
What a bloody fine lot,
Fred Karno's sent today!

Top: Northumberland Fusiliers Football Team at Cambois during the winter of 1914-15. *Middle:* With both professional and amateur footballers joining the ranks of the Northumberland Fusiliers Service Battalions all the Newcastle Battalions had keen and competitive football teams while in training and even when they went overseas. *Right:* Other sports such as boxing were also encouraged to toughen up the men (FMN).

Above: Got the equipment, best test it out on
Next page, top: The men of 12 Platoon, C Company, 10
Northumberland Fusiliers. Bottom: 18th Battalion, Northumberland
Tyneside Pioneers)

18TH NORTHUMBERLAND FUSILIERS

arch, 1915.
) Battalion,
ottom: (1st
war 1915.

45

The famous 'Harder than Hammers' Tyneside Scottish recruiting poster produced by Andrew Reid & Co 1914.

"SCOTLAND FOR EVER."

TYNESIDE SCOTTISH BRIGADE

" Harder than Hammers "

SCOTSMEN ON TYNESIDE

are given the opportunity to defend their Country's honour by

ENROLLING NOW

in this fine Brigade which is quickly being filled with the **Toughest, Hardest and Best Tyneside Fighting Men.**

AGE LIMIT 19 TO 45

HEIGHT, 5ft. 3ins. CHEST, 34ins.

Central Recruiting Office:

9 Grainger Street West, Newcastle

BRANCHES IN MOST TYNESIDE TOWNS

ONE MAN TO-DAY WORTH THREE IN THREE MONTHS.

GOD SAVE THE KING.

Andrew Reid & Company, Limited.

Tyneside Scottish

'Harder than Hammers'
    Motto of the Tyneside Scottish

The first attempt to raise a Tyneside Scottish Battalion began in September 1914 but acceptance by the War Office did not come and they lost most of their initial recruits to other battalions. The main sticking point had been that the War Office was not prepared to allow the Tyneside Scottish to wear kilts. As recruitment began to slow down nationally in October 1914 it was clear Kitchener had heard of the desire to raise a Tyneside Scottish battalion and when Lord Chancellor Haldane came to Newcastle and addressed huge patriotic meetings he brought a message stating that Lord Kitchener had spoken with him and he declared 'We are going to give you a Scottish Battalion here.'

The sanction was finally received from the War Office on 14 October 1914 and the first recruiting office for the Tyneside Scottish opened at Sir Walter Scott's shop at 17 Grainger Street, Newcastle. Others soon followed at Gosforth, North Shields, Wallsend, Hebburn, Jarrow, South Shields, Prudhoe, Blaydon, Durham City and Crawcrook.

Initially, while they waited for their uniforms, recruits were issued with blue and white cord worn around one shoulder and then Royal Stuart tartan arm bands emblazoned with a white patch bearing the letters 'TS'. Permission was granted by the War Office for the wearing of a distinctive headdress in the form of a

Next page, top: All ranks of 2nd Battalion Tyneside Scottish (2 Battalion, Northumberland Fusiliers) on the Pastures, Alnwick. *Bottom:* The Pipes and Drums of 2nd Battalion Tyneside Scotti Battalion, Northumberland Fusiliers). The pipers of the 1st Bat the Northumbrian 'Shepherd's Plaid' but the 2nd Battalion wo Campbell of Loudon tartan as seen here (FMN).

Glengarry and the issue of cut-away tunics, so distinctive to Scottish troops, was made to battalion's pipers. A cap badge unique to the Tyneside Scottish designed by Major Innes-Hopkins was also permitted but still there was no overall permission to wear kilts. However, with the enlistment of seven pipers for the pipe band, it was decided only they should be allowed to wear kilts of the distinctive black and white check Shepherds plaid associated with Northumberland. As a little aside, when the 3rd Tyneside Scottish established their corps of drums it was led by Drum Major Leonard Godber aged just eighteen, he was the youngest soldier to hold that rank in the British Army.

A recruiting poster for the battalion, headed by a full colour representation of the flags of the allies and displaying the motto 'Harder than Hammers' for the first time was produced free of charge by Andrew Reid & Co. Recruiting was brisk and a full battalion of 1,200 men was completed by 25 October. So great was the demand the War Office gave its assent for a second battalion of Tyneside Scottish to be raised the following day. This battalion was complete by 5 November, then a Third by 11 November and after the Fourth was sanctioned on 16 November it was full within twenty-four hours, thus the Tyneside Scottish Brigade was created and the 1st-4th Tyneside Scottish were adopted as 20th -23rd (Service) Battalions, Northumberland Fusiliers.

The original idea was that the Tyneside Scottish should be a battalion made up of Scots by birth or direct descent but so many who joined wanted to bring their Geordie pals who would joke that they had joined for 'the craic ah bein' a kiltie.' The volunteers had come from across the county but the three-hundred men who volunteered for the Tyneside Scottish from Bedlington Colliery is a truly remarkable contribution and the

Colour of 2nd Battalion, Tyneside Scottish was laid up there after the war and hangs in St Cuthbert's Church, Bedlington to this day.

After being billeted and beginning their training in Newcastle the first real camp for all battalions of the Tyneside Scottish to gather together to train and truly become a fighting brigade was to be at Alnwick, and they went there in true military style. An advance party was sent on 26 January and the rest of the 20th Battalion, Northumberland Fusiliers (1st Battalion, Tyneside Scottish) set out from Newcastle to march forty miles to the camp at Alnwick on 29 January 1915. Given a fine send off attended by a large crowd outside the Town Hall the march was completed in two stages; the first leg was from Newcastle to Seaton Burn where they would halt to rest and eat lunch then on to Morpeth where they would stay for the night. Led by the pipe band, with occasional breaks for the pipers filled with tunes provided by an unofficial mouth organ band and songs from the ranks they marched on through inclement weather conditions of hail and rain only occasionally punctuated by welcome breaks of sunshine. Nonetheless every village on route turned out to wave flags and cheer to the boys as they passed through.

The accommodation allotted to some of the lads for the overnight stop at Morpeth came as a bit of shock – a stable! So a number of them who lived in the surrounding villages took pals with them and spent the night in comfortable beds at home – sharing four or five to a bed and they came back on the 6am train to Morpeth ready for the march out at 9am.

Ten miles out the Battalion halted at midday in a small field near Felton where barrels of beer had been put upon the stocks and the boys were greatly cheered by this halt before the final leg of the march to Alnwick.

Right: The Reserve Battalion of the Tyneside Scottish arriving at Barnard Castle, January 1916.

As the footsore Tyneside Scottish boys approached the town (many by that time, were marching on a bed of blisters on the soles of their feet and in quite some pain) they were met by the band and drums of the 'Newcastle Commercials' 16th (Service) Battalion, who had been at their section of Alnwick camp since early December 1914. (The 'Commericals' had, however, made their original journey to the camp by train.) They all marched in column to the railway station where the pipes and drums struck up again and played them into and through the town to cheers from the crowds of local people who lined their route. Pte. Tom Easton would recall:

'...with this fresh inspiration, we put up a splendid show as we clattered over the cobbles and in through the narrow gateway of the town (Bondgate)...we felt the spirit of achievement and forgot the pain of our feet and aching limbs.'

It was a day that would be remembered well by all who were there for years afterwards.

The rest of the Tyneside Scottish Battalions arrived at Alnwick over the ensuing months until all were gathered there by May 1915.

Pte. Tom Easton sums up the way the men felt from that time, despite the training being intensive and the route marches frequent:

'Many of us felt now at home for no more beautiful setting could have been picked for our camp, nestling quietly on the wooded slope facing the great stronghold of past days, Alnwick Castle, with the River Aln flowing quietly in between...some of the most pleasant days of our four years existence as an infantry battalion of the redoubtable British Army.'

The Tyneside Scottish Brigade moved later that year to their first canvas camp at Hornsea, Yorkshire, Lugershall and then Windmill Hill on Salisbury Plain. Their last camp at home was to be at Longbridge Deverill just outside Warminster where they were formed with the Tyneside Irish and other brigades and Divisional Corps to create the 34th Division and proceeded to France from there leaving Southampton bound for Le Havre on 10 January 1916.

Some early volunteers for the Tyneside Irish, proudly wearing the green arm bands given to them to signify they had enlisted.

Tyneside Irish

There has never been a time where Ireland could claim an abundance of work and the industrial revolution in Britain during the early nineteenth century proved to be a draw for many Irishmen and their families to leave their native shores and seek a better life in Britain and beyond. Newcastle has had an Irish community since the early 1800s and it expanded steadily until the coming of the railways in the 1830s when hundreds more Irishmen came over to work as 'navvies' in the construction of the new 'iron roads.' When depression and the horrific Irish potato famine hit in 1846 thousands more followed.

Many came to the North East in the knowledge the area offered good chances of finding unskilled and semi skilled work in mines, shipyards and other industries, they took whatever job they could. By the time Britain hit its industrial apogee in the 1850s and 60s it was estimated some two million Irish born people or those of Irish descent were living in Great Britain and the Irish population of the North East was the fourth highest in the country, behind London, Liverpool and Manchester. Although the work was hard, the Irish soon found the life they could lead in and around Newcastle, although far from the lap of luxury, was better than in many other industrial areas and the instances of sectarian violence were far less frequent then elsewhere. Irish journalist and popular M.P. T. P. O'Connor wrote in *Irish Heroes in the War* (1917):

'*Of the many asylums to which the Irish fled after the great exodus of the forties, there was none in which, owing to many circumstances, they were able to ultimately find more favourable surroundings than the Tyneside. It was partly due to the fact that this is so great a centre of the mining industry and that these Irish exiles were able to find employment immediately, which, though hard in conditions – and harder then than now – was welcome to men of stalwart frames and great need. ..I think, in saying that the mine has something of the same reconciling spirit of the battlefield: common danger makes comrades and brothers of those who before had been apart by race or creed or class.*'

In those same mines many Irish miners became stalwart supporters of Trade Union causes fighting for better pay and conditions, many of them became Union officials too.

The Irish communities or 'colonies' along the banks of the Tyne in Sandgate and Castle Steps in Newcastle built their own Roman Catholic churches (St. Mary's Church, now St. Mary's Cathedral was built in 1842-44) and chapels complete with adjoining church rooms that soon became hubs for community groups, bands, schools and entertainments. Indeed, the first 'Irish Club' in Britain was founded by a committee in a rented room at the top of Clayton Street in 1871.

In 1914, concerns were being raised in the Irish community over the conditions new recruits were being subjected to, especially poor accommodation. There were also fears that Ireland would not get the credit it deserved for supplying so many men to the colours and since there was a Tyneside Scottish Battalion being formed in Newcastle, it was felt by significant numbers in the Irish community that there should be a Tyneside Irish Battalion too. An open letter signed by the

committee was published in the *Newcastle Evening Chronicle* on 12 September 1914 in which it stated '*The idea of regiments of 'Pals', which has received the sanction of the War Office, and has proved such a huge success all over the country, is a good one, and in order to give it our full support and do our utmost to assist the country in this terrific struggle, we suggest that an Irish Regiment be formed on Tyneside, which Irishmen of all classes and denominations can join.*'

The letter concluded by stating that a meeting to promote the idea was to be held at Collingwood Hall, The Irish National Centre the following day at 3pm and there it was resolved that just such a battalion would be raised. Temporary offices were taken in Collingwood Street and less than a week later some six hundred men had offered themselves as recruits for the Tyneside Irish.

The Tyneside Irish Battalion offered to become part of the 16th (Irish) Division that was then being formed in Southern Ireland. Their offer, however, was rebuffed by the Division's Commander Lieut. Gen. L. W. Parsons whose high handed reply stated he wanted no 'slum birds' in his Division and on 20 September it was announced communication had been received from the Army Council that approval had not been granted for a Tyneside Irish Battalion to be formed.

Many of those who answered that original call for volunteers joined other battalions of the Northumberland Fusiliers, Hussars and Durham Light Infantry but all was not lost. War Minister Kitchener and Lord Haldane were only too aware of the value of having locally raised battalions and during his visit to Newcastle on 10 October 1914 Haldane declared that there would be Scottish, Irish and a second Commercial

The first major recruiting advertisement to appear in a newspaper for the Tyneside Irish, October 1914 and the eye-catching recruiting poster for the Tyneside Irish, 1914.

battalions raised in Newcastle. Thus with the extant Commercials Battalion the intention was to create four Battalions for Kitchener's Army, a veritable 'Tyneside Brigade' no less! War Office sanction for the Lord Mayor, Councillor Johnstone Wallace (a fine Irish gentleman from County Derry) to raise the three battalions arrived on 15 October 1914.

The immediate problem was that the funds for raising the battalions were not immediately available from the War Office. It is thanks to the work of the Chamber of Commerce and a generous donation of £10,000 (equivalent to £1,040,000 today) from Mr. Joseph Cowen of Stella Hall, Blaydon that the Battalions were raised. Cowen's father, the late Joseph Cowen had made his money making bricks, had been a radical politician, Member of Parliament for Newcastle, sympathiser to the Irish Nationalist cause and owner of the *Newcastle Daily Chronicle*. Mr Cowen Snr. had left a legacy for Newcastle in so many ways and his son was determined to carry on that good work. His gift meant the raising of the new Tyneside Scottish and Irish battalions could proceed with every confidence.

The Tariff Reform Offices in Collingwood Buildings were turned into recruiting rooms for the Tyneside Irish and the ground floor of the Town Hall became temporary accommodation. Recruiting kicked-off in earnest with a parade that set off from the monument to Joseph Cowen (senior) on Westgate Road, with the Birtley St. Joseph's brass band at the head leading them through the district. Folks cheered, flags were waved and men joined up.

The great and the good came to speak at recruiting meetings including T. P. O'Connor M.P. and the Earl of Donoughmore. Concerts were held and whole pages were given over to adverts calling 'Irishmen to Arms' and 'Irishmen for the Battle Line' accompanied by

pictures of famous military heroes of Irish descent appealing for men to join the Tyneside Irish – there was even an application form to cut out and send in for you to join! The Ladies Committee was established to provide comforts, extra suits, shirts, socks and warm winter clothing for the men of the battalion. But for the new recruits in the meantime a green cloth arm band had to suffice to identify them as volunteers for the battalion.

In the early days training parades of the Tyneside Irish were usually held in Eldon Square where they would fall in and form fours with the tall and impressive Major

THE EAST COAST OUTRAGE.
Will You Take It Lying Down?
IF NOT, JOIN THE COLOURS AT ONCE.
Our Strategic Frontier is on the Continent.
THERE ONLY WILL TERMS OF PEACE BE DICTATED.

Tyneside Irish Brigade.

I desire to join the Tyneside Irish Brigade. Please have my name placed on the list, and I agree to be attested when called upon to do so.

Signed—
Full Name
Address

Age   Height   Chest Measurement
Married or Single   Date

This Form to be returned to—
THE SECRETARIES (J. Mulcahy, Esq., and Gerald Stoney, F.R.S., Esq.)
Tyneside Irish Brigade,
6 and 7, Collingwood Buildings, Collingwood Street,
Newcastle-on-Tyne.

PAY COMMENCES FROM ATTESTATION.

Never backward in coming forwards, the adverts suggest you join the Tyneside Irish to avenge the bombardment of Scarborough, Whitby and Hartlepool, December 1914.

Joe Prior in command. Then they would march off to the Town Moor to begin their day's training accompanied by their drum and fife band playing such tunes as *Tipperaray* and *The Harp that once through Tara's Halls*.

Recruiting Offices for the Tyneside Irish were eventually opened across the North East, a further donation of £5,000 (equivalent to £520,000 today) for unforeseen expenses was made by Joseph Cowen and better accommodation was found at Dunn's Buildings on Friar Street. Recruits kept coming along and the one battalion grew into two, three, four battalions and thus by November 1914 the creation of a Tyneside Irish Brigade was well within sight. On 12 January 1915 it was announced that the Tyneside Irish Brigade, five thousand five hundred men strong had been completed. The finishing touch was suggested by Colonel Myles Emmet Byrne, a band of *Pipes of Erin*, and the Brigade soon had the only complete band of Irish war-pipes in the country. On 11 March 1915 it was those pipes with green ribbons fluttering off the drones that led the 1st Battalion, Tyneside Irish as they marched out of Eldon Square to the railway station, bound for their first real military camp at Alnwick.

It should be noted, that like the Tyneside Scottish, the Tyneside Irish Battalions were part of The Northumberland Fusiliers:

1st Battalion, Tyneside Irish – 24th Battalion, Northumberland Fusiliers
2nd Battalion, Tyneside Irish – 25th Battalion, Northumberland Fusiliers
3rd Battalion, Tyneside Irish – 26th Battalion, Northumberland Fusiliers
4th Battalion, Tyneside Irish – 27th Battalion, Northumberland Fusiliers

The Tyneside Irish Brigade celebrated their very first St. Patrick's Day on 17 March 1915. The 1st Battalion celebrated at their new camp in Alnwick, the 2nd Battalion in Birtley and the 4th Battalion at their new quarters at Raby Street Schools. The 3rd Battalion marched from their quarters at the Sunbeam Buildings, Gateshead to parade at Eldon Square where every soldier was presented with a shamrock sprig by Miss Fitzgerald the Lady Mayoress followed by her sister Miss M. Fitzgerald who presented every man with a packet of cigarettes as the band played a selection of Irish airs. The men saluted and fastened the shamrock to their hats. Although the rain came down the parades carried on. A total of 4,300 men received shamrocks at four locations and it was a day that many would remember with affection and pride for the rest of their lives.

After Alnwick and a very brief stay at Haltwhistle the Brigade began to assemble at Woolsington Park, Ponteland in May 1915. While there they were designated to be the 103rd Brigade of the 34th Division under the command of Major General Edward Charles Ingouville-Williams, a man who earned the respect of the men and came to be known to them as 'Inky Bill.' In August 1915 the War Office took over the Brigade and relieved the Tyneside Irish Committee of any further responsibilities or financial obligations but of course the Committee kept in touch and maintained a keen interest in the progress of their boys. Over the last days of August 1915 the Tyneside Irish Brigade entrained for Windmill Hill Camp on Salisbury Plain. After the weather took a turn for the worse and their camp suffered regular flooding the Brigade moved to nearby Sutton Veny where they celebrated Christmas and New Year. After over a year in training and just as the men began to wonder if they would ever be sent for active service the Tyneside Irish Brigade was mobilized to serve in France on 4 January 1916. The Brigade was divided in two for embarkation, the 26th Battalion and 27th Battalions leaving from Folkestone on 10 and 11 January respectively, landing at Boulogne and 24th and 25th Battalions travelling from Southampton and landing at Le Havre on 11 January. The Battalions travelled in trains to St. Omer where they were reunited and proceeded from there to the front.

Originally worn on the epaulettes on the jacket with battalion number above and the brass letters 'N.F.' below. The Tyneside Irish badge can be seen on photographs to have been removed from the shoulders to be worn as collar badges from about 1917 but it was never worn as a cap badge. *Below:* Soldiers from the Tyneside Irish during the winter of 1914-15 (FMN).

The first day of the Somme

It is often forgotten that our Newcastle raised battalions had been in France for about six months before July 1916 during which time they had done their stints occupying front line trenches, forming wiring and occasional raiding parties, sniping and engaging with the enemy. Having seen their mates killed by snipers, 'Minniewerfer' mortar shells and artillery fire many of our boys had become frustrated with the stalemate of the trenches and wanted to get to grips with the enemy in a much vaunted 'Big Push' to break the deadlock on the Western Front.

Nine battalions of the Northumberland Fusiliers went 'over the top' into action on 1 July 1916 the first day of the Somme, namely 16th (Service) Battalion, the Tyneside Scottish and the Tyneside Irish Brigades - every one of them a battalion raised in Newcastle.

Tragically, the 16th (Service) Battalion would sustain numerous casualties before they even went over the top. The Battalion moved off in platoons from Knight's Redoubt bound for the front line trenches of the Somme on the evening of 30 June making their way via Martinsart, Aveluy Wood and Black Horse Bridge.

The Historical Record of the 16th Battalion evocatively picks up the story:

'The road all the way was crowded with troops, guns, ammunition columns and regimental transport; for miles the route was just one mass of men, horses and vehicles. It seemed chaotic; yet all moved forward with one definite aim. Nearer and nearer to the trenches the troops marched: speech was almost an impossibility, the very air vibrated with the perpetual cannonade. Enemy guns were searching the roads but the 16th reached the entrance to the communication trench without mishap. Many casualties occurred before the battalion reached its battle position, where it relieved the 2nd Inniskillings at 2.30am. The front line was not recognisable, so badly damaged was it. Still raged the frightful shell-fire: It was not a case of odd shells, or even salvoes at intervals. The air was thick with flying metal, shrieking fiends of death.'

When the men of the 16th Battalion reached the forward trenches A and B Companies occupied the front line from Skinner Street to Maison Grise Sap as they were to lead the attack with C Company in support occupying two communication trenches (two platoons in Hamilton Avenue and a further two in Gourock Street) and D Company in reserve in the second line (Gemmel Trench). The area they held faced the German trenches built deep into the high ground of Thiepval Ridge where Thiepval Memorial to the missing now stands.

The Historical Record of the 16th Battalion continues:

'Zero hour was at 7.30 am on 1st July, and for five hours the battalion stood to, crowded into the trenches. All through the night the enemy fired steadily and the list of casualties rapidly increased. The protecting barrage was to be put down at 7.30am. In a war of miracles and mysteries, these screens of bursting shells were unique. An animate curtain, it swayed viciously

The explosion at Hawthorn Ridge on 1 July 1916. A larger explosion was detonated at 'Lochnagar' near La Boiselle, to the right of the planned attack area of 34th Division and a second slightly smaller explosion was at Y Sap on the left flank. The chalk bed blasted up there saw the area not only covered in debris but clouded in dust which covered the ground like snow when it settled.

before the advancing troops and advanced with them over the ground. Where fringes flicked the earth it seemed impossible that any human could live.

Punctual to a second, the barrage fell, as if from the skies. The leading waves scrambled over the top of the parapet but the impossible had happened. Human beings had lived through that awful fire and from their machine guns, cunningly concealed in concrete emplacements they poured a murderous leaden stream of bullets into our men. As the barrage moved behind the enemy front line, the Huns stood upon their parapet and invited the men to 'Come on' picking them off with accurate rifle fire. So intense was the enemy shooting that our leading waves were forced to lie down. 'C' Company which had moved up to the front line, saw this, and attempted to reinforce but suffered heavily as soon as the men got over the top.'

'D' Company and Battalion HQ moved forward to the front line and 'D' Company was ordered to advance but the first platoon met the same fate as the leading waves as they went over the top.

L/Cpl. Stan Henderson of High Heaton, Newcastle was the runner for the Battalion C.O, Colonel W.H. Ritson and had to stay close by him as they moved from 16th Battalion's dug-out H.Q. to the front line and saw the growing agitation of his commanding officer first-hand. Years later Stan would recall:

'It was suicide, a massacre; you could hear the wounded shouting – the Colonel paced helplessly back and forth and, eventually, tears streaming down his cheeks, cried: "My God, my God, my men, my men. We had to restrain him from going over the top himself.'

With carnage suffered by the first platoon of D Company enough was enough. The remainder were ordered to stand fast and man the fire steps of the front line to give covering fire on the enemy that were still visible standing or kneeling on the parapets of their trenches. Still the toll of casualties increased among the men out in No Man's Land. Orders were received late in the day that the battalion was to be relieved by the 16th Battalion, Lancashire Fusiliers.

In the 16th (Service) Battalion Northumberland Fusiliers War Diary, tributes were paid to the battalion stretcher-bearers and the men of 'A' Company of the 2nd Battalion, Royal Inniskilling Fusiliers who did such brave work carrying many of the wounded back to British lines from No Man's Land. Every man was worthy of praise, the Diary continued:

'The men of the attacking Companies moved forward like one man until the murderous fire of the enemy's machine guns forced them to halt. Not a man waivered and after nightfall we found in several places, straight lines of ten or twelve dead or badly wounded as if the Platoons had just been dressed for parade.'

It was only remnants of the battalion, numbering some eight officers and 279 other ranks marched into the Bluff, to the north of Black Horse Bridge at 1.30am on 2 July 1916.

Map of the Somme showing the British advance from 1 July up to 27 September.

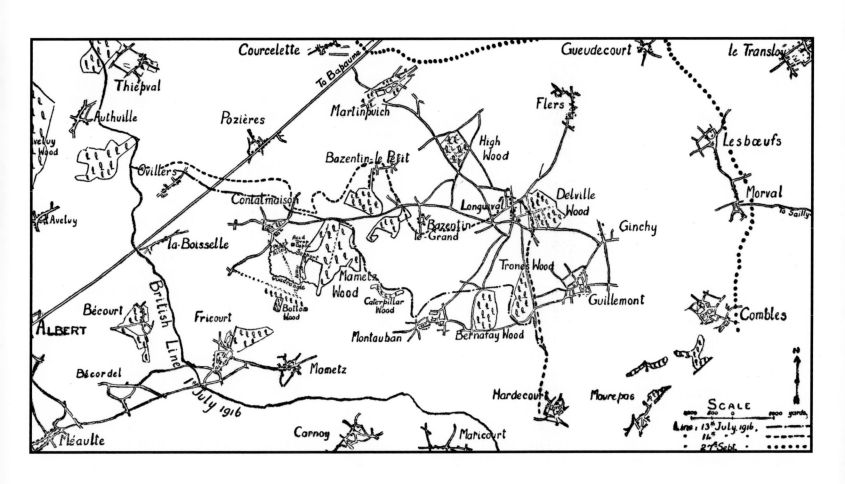

The Tyneside Scottish on the Somme

The plan for the 34th Division was to throw the full weight of the twelve infantry battalions of the Division against La Boiselle. The Tyneside Scottish Brigade was to lead the attack astride the La Boiselle salient to take the German strongpoint of the village of La Boiselle from the sides rather than headlong. The men of the 18th (Service) Battalion, Northumberland Fusiliers (Pioneers) would maintain the forward dumps of Mills bombs, rifle grenades, Stokes shells, ammunition and rations in the middle ground in an area known as 'The Glory Hole' as well as helping to run said supplies and deploy troops to dig mortar pits or provide manual labour when required.

It was intended that the attacking columns of the Tyneside Scottish were to advance either side of the village then send in bombing parties, supported by Lewis gun teams and Stokes mortar parties, to clear it out as the columns pressed on to the next objective. The 1st and 4th Battalions to the left were to start at zero hour, 7.30 advancing almost side by side while the 2nd Battalion to the right, immediately supported by the 3rd Battalion following in the same order, would have to wait two minutes to allow the debris of the huge 'Lochnagar' mine to descend without hitting the men. No Man's Land was much narrower in this area than on the left where the other great explosion at 'Y Sap' was to be detonated. When the mines were blown the blast not only shot up huge quantities of earth but also huge clouds of chalk from the bed below coating a wide area around the explosion with a blanket of white giving the appearance of snow.

To reach their first objective in the attack the men of the 1st and 4th Tyneside Scottish would have to cross 880 yards of crater riddled No Man's Land to reach the first German front line trenches. Their second objective was the German defences on the west of Contalmaison and the third, a line running east of Contalmaison towards to east of Pozieres.

The orders given before the advance, as recorded in the War Diary of the 4th Tyneside Scottish were quite specific:

'Once the attack is launched it must be pressed forward at all costs until the final objective of the Battalion is reached. The extreme importance of a resolute advance must be clearly impressed on all ranks and the advance must continue regardless of whether other units or our flanks are held up or delayed.'

The problem was that the German listening post 'Moritz' had intercepted a fragment of orders for the 34th Division for the following day and had notified the men of the 110 and 111 Reserve Infantry Regiments to prepare for the attack and to deploy their machine gun crews as soon as the barrage lifted on that warm and sunny morning of 1 July 1916.

Pte. George Charlton of the Tyneside Scottish wrote home about his experiences on the First Day of the Somme :

'We held the trenches during the eight days' bombardments previous to going over the top, which was enough to break any man down...I was up all Friday night helping in the issue of stuff and about 4.00am had to go with hot tea and bacon for the men's

breakfasts. At 7.00am we were told to prepare for a big mine going off and at 7.20 up it went. What a sight! Earth and smoke were flying heavenwards and we were nearly shaken to pieces. The waiting to get away was awful. When orders came to advance, what a change there was! Every man rushed to the ladders to get over. You shook hands with a pal, wished him the best of luck, and over the top. The German artillery was awful but some smoking tabs, others cheering and all smiling over we went, the pipers playing 'The Campbells are Coming.' Some poor souls were killed before we got away but we took no notice, as we must get on. On all sides men were falling but on we went over our lines into 'No Man's Land' which was the ground between the opposing lines. It was simply awful, but you had to take no notice. We were also catching the German machine-gun fire, which made things worse, and the ground was simply ploughed up with shells.

What a good job our artillery had blown their wire to pieces, so we could get over canny and mount the first line German trench. How anyone lived to get over I don't know. The first thing I saw was our bombers at work in the German dug-outs. After getting our wind we prepared to take the second line. I don't know what I felt like. I think no-one was in their right senses; the sights were enough to turn anyone's brain. All I seem to remember was jumping over the parapet and yelling at the top of my voice.

No sooner did we show ourselves than the machine guns were opened on us. Men fell on all sides but we managed to get the second line. Then came the order to take the third line, and over the top we went again but the machine gun fire was awful. When about five yards from the trenches I staggered and fell into a shell hole where two of our men were. They asked where I was hit but I was only dazed and they left me. That night I

Pipe Major John Wilson, 1st Tyneside Scottish, played his Company over the parapet and across 'No Man's Land' amid a hail of fire on 1 July 1916 (FMN).

The notification letter the family of Sgt. David Goodall received after he was admitted to the 10th General Hospital at Rouen on 2 July 1916 with a gun shot wound to his left shoulder (FMN).

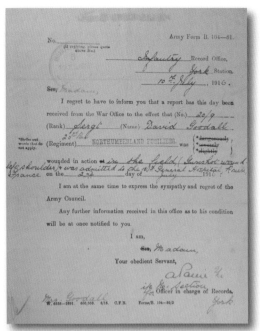

found out the reason why I fell. A piece of shrapnel went right through my haversack, then through a leather purse, through my ration bag among my biscuits, through the side of a tin of Oxo cubes and out of the lid but never hurt me. I lay there and dare not move. If I showed my head a bullet came whistling back. I stayed there until it became unbearable, so I decided to crawl back to the second line.'

George Charlton was fortunate in that the barbed wire had been cut where he was crossing, in many other areas it had only been cut in places leaving dangerous gaps for the advancing troops to funnel through and be picked off by machine gunners.

Every company of the Tyneside Scottish had been played over by their pipers, they marched towards the gun fire until they fell dead or wounded. An unnamed officer from the 8th Division who attacked the neighbouring Ovilliers spur on 1 July gave an interview to a reporter in which he stated:

'The pluckiest thing I ever saw was a piper of the Tyneside Scottish playing his company over the parapet in the attack on the German trenches near Albert. The Tynesiders were on our right and as their officers gave the signal to advance I saw the piper – I think he was the Pipe Major – jump out of the trench and march

straight over No Man's Land towards the German lines. The tremendous rattle of machine gun and rifle fire, which the enemy at once opened on us and completely drowned the sound of his pipes. But it was obvious he was playing as though he would burst the bag and just faintly through the din we heard the mighty shout his comrades gave as they swarmed after him. How he escaped death I can't understand for the ground was literally ploughed up by the hail of bullets.'

Pipe Major John Wilson was awarded the Military Medal for his 'conspicuous bravery and devotion to duty' on 1 July 1916

The minute the Tyneside Scottish left their trenches they encountered deadly cross machine gun fire from Orvilliers on the left, short range machine gun fire from La Boiselle and its trenches on the right and also suffered shelling. The two leading battalions of the Tyneside Scottish pressed on gallantly but were decimated before they reached the front line enemy trenches. In a matter of about 10 minutes some 80 per cent of the leading battalions had become casualties, 15 out of the 16 company commanders were casualties and many senior NCOs had also been killed or wounded. One old soldier remarked, 'it took twelve months to build our battalion but just twelve minutes to destroy it.'

Incredibly, some men made it through to the forward objectives such as Contalmaison but could not hold them after the battalions had suffered such casualties to achieve them.

The 34th Division suffered the worst casualties of any Division on the First Day of the Somme. The Tyneside Scottish Battalions were reduced to about half their size. In total over 2,280 officers and men of the Tyneside Scottish Brigade were either dead or wounded after that one day of action.

The Tyneside Irish on the Somme

The duty of the Tyneside Irish Brigade on the First Day of the Somme was to press home the attack on the Germans positions spearheaded by the Tyneside Scottish to the north and adjoining the village of La Boiselle.

Starting from trenches near the two small hills christened Tara and Usna by the Tyneside Irish, they crossed the brow of the hill and were visible above the horizon. They then had hundreds of yards of open country to traverse before they reached the British front line and suffered early casualties from German rifle, machine gun and shell fire while making their way there from the assembly trenches.

Each company advanced in column of platoons leaving one hundred and fifty paces interval between them, the regular lines, dressings and unshakable discipline, almost as if they were on a parade square, was remarked upon with awe by all who witnessed it.

The 18th Battalion (Pioneers) had a good view of the advance of the Tyneside Irish from their 'Glory Hole' and Lieut. Col. John Shakespear records in their battalion history:

'It was a lovely morning, bright sun and very little wind. The guns kept up an incessant roar but above us hovered a lark quite undisturbed. The mines went off and a few minutes later the 103rd (Tyneside Irish) Brigade began coming over the hill in beautifully regular lines, dressing and intervals maintained as well as on a ceremonial parade. Everyone felt proud of that lot of Tynesiders.'

Lieut. James Hately, of the Tyneside Irish, wrote with some considerable pride to his brother:

'The Irish were "topping!" What a glorious sight it was for us to see the men we'd trained going forward as steadily as human beings possibly could, and they never kept a better line on manoeuvres than they did that day. I have met officers of the Machine Gun Corps and an R.E. officer, who said it was simply thrilling to see those "Tyneside Irish chaps" as they were referred to, coming through and past the other troops (as per programme). I could see some - not my own men from where I lay (I lay where I fell for two hours, the pain was so great and the machine guns were still centred on the area where I was), and I could see the gaps that shell-bursts, shrapnel, machine guns, and all the damned tortures of war tore in their ranks.

I could see men stumble and fall headlong or see others go up in the air, but still the remainder went steadily forward, till I lost them when they crested the hill. I think they were "ripping." I started off with a cigarette well alight, officers and men exchanging cheery "good lucks" and "cheer'os." Most of us were laughing though I own I felt sorry for the poor chaps, as so many would never see home again.

As for myself, it never occurred to me that I should be hit, for you know how optimistic I have always been. We kept up a running fire of chaff, and got a good reply too, as Irish wit will out. Some of the fellows were very quiet, but none the less determined. This (moving up and down talking) was before starting, and when the guns were at their heaviest. Well, we started off with a yell and went steadily on for about 200 yards before we felt their fire. Then it was a hail of lead, with the ground heaving up in front, behind and all around us. It was terrible, and yet there wasn't a pale face to be seen. When I fell they were excited. When they reached the Boche lines, as I'm told they did, to the sorrow of Fritz, they must have been mad. I wish the people who have sons and husbands who fell could know of this. They ought to. *It is some satisfaction to know that the Tyneside Irish did well that day.'*

The Tyneside Irish, like the Tyneside Scottish, were played 'over the top' into action by their pipers. One of the pipers, according to an account in *Irish Heroes in the War* (1919) was seen marching ahead of the men, 'piping, through a storm of bullets which were wounding and killing his comrades all around him, until he himself fell among the wounded.' One of the tunes recalled played on that day by the Irish pipers was the old Irish patriotic song *The Minstrel Boy* by Thomas Moore (1779-1852) set to the melody of *The Moreen*, the words on lips and in the minds of the men who heard it were only too apt:

"The minstrel boy to the war is gone,
In the ranks of death you'll find him;
His father's sword he has girded on,
And his wild harp slung behind him;
"Land of Song!" said the warrior bard,
"Though all the world betrays thee,
One sword, at least, thy rights shall guard,
One faithful harp shall praise thee!"

Of your Charity
Pray for the Repose of the Soul of

Pte. Michael Clarke,
26th North.'d Fusiliers,
The dearly beloved Son of Mary and the late
Patrick Clarke.

Who was killed in Action in France on

JULY 1st, 1916,

AGED 34 YEARS.

Fortified by all the Rites of Holy Church,

On whose Soul, sweet Jesus, have mercy.

The dearly beloved Husband of Georgina Clarke.

BEHOLD, O good and most sweet JESUS, I cast myself upon my knees in Thy sight and with all the fervour of my soul, I pray and beseech Thee to vouchsafe to impress upon my heart lively sentiments of Faith, Hope, and Charity, with true sorrow for my sins, and a most firm purpose of amendment : while, with great affection and grief of soul, I ponder within myself and mentally contemplate Thy five wounds, having before my eyes what Thou didst say of Thyself, O good JESUS, by the Prophet David : "They have pierced My hands and My feet, they have numbered all My bones."

A Plenary Indulgence may be gained, on the usual conditions, by reciting the foregoing prayer before an image of Christ crucified. It is also applicable to the souls in Purgatory.

JESUS, meek and humble of heart, make my heart like unto Thine. 300 days' Ind.

GvRI

HE whom this scroll commemorates was numbered among those who, at the call of King and Country, left all that was dear to them, endured hardness, faced danger, and finally passed out of the sight of men by the path of duty and self-sacrifice, giving up their own lives that others might live in freedom.

Let those who come after see to it that his name be not forgotten.

Pte. John Elliott McMillan
Northumberland Fusiliers

Previous page: One of the most famous and iconic images of the Battle of the Somme is captured here in the advance of the Tyneside Irish, on the morning of 1 July 1916.

This page, clockwise from top left: 1) 'In Memoriam' card for Pte. Michael Clarke 3rd Battalion, Tyneside Irish (26th Battalion, Northumberland Fusiliers), who was killed in action on 1 July 1916 (FMN). 2) Memorial Scroll sent to the parents of Pte. John Elliott McMillan, who was killed in action on the Somme while serving with 2nd Battalion, Tyneside Scottish on 1 July 1916. He was just 19 years old (FMN). 3) Pte. Michael Clarke (FMN).

In addition to the hail of machine gun and rifle fire there was a considerable artillery barrage at three places on the line of advance but despite all this the forward movement was maintained until only a few scattered soldiers were left standing.

Bomber Edward Dyke of the Tyneside Irish wrote an evocative account of the action to his brother:

'I am at present at the base hospital. I was put under the X Rays to see if my skull was fractured or whether there was anything in my head. I was wounded on the first day of the big advance. My Division led the attack in our particular part. The scene baffles description. The gates of hell were opened, and we accepted the invitation to enter. The coolness and courage of the Tyneside Irish was marvellous, not a man wavered. We all had a heavy load to carry, a pick or shovel down the back of the straps, haversack, equipment, rifle with bayonet fixed, and I, as a bomber, a bag of grenades – enough to put out a couple of companies of Germans. How anyone got to the German lines I don't know, but we managed it, or rather some of us. Machine-guns mowed us down, shells were bursting all around us, and our own artillery pouring shells into the Germans. It was 7.30 a.m. when we went over, and broad daylight. Two mines were exploded in the German lines; they were like earthquakes. What cowards the Germans are. Once among them with the bayonet and they scream for mercy!

We had to face the Prussian Imperial Regiments, men over 6 feet tall, backed up by some Prussian Guards. I also saw some Bavarians. Later I got hit with a piece of shell and the earth left me. When I recovered I was blind with the blood, and wiping my eyes, I saw a large shell hole which I managed to reach, and threw myself into it. Taking out my field dressing, I bandaged my head. The return to safety was as bad as the charge. We came

down a slope which I had now to ascend. Machine guns were rattling, and Germans snipers from an opposite hill were picking off the wounded

I fell unconscious for the second time, but on the way to safety I managed to bandage up four or five wounded by taking the field dressing from the pockets of some of the dead. Many would not leave the shell holes to try to get back, but I was losing blood, and if the Germans successfully counter-attacked and I was still there, I knew my fate.

How I got back is a mystery. My steel helmet, the doctor says, saved my life. I would have had my brain knocked in if I had not been wearing it.

Later I heard the battalion roll call in a small trench. Poor old Tyneside Irish! We made the sacrifice to pave the way for the advance. It has proved a success. The village, which was our objective, has fallen. Let's hope it will finish the war. May God comfort the widows and fatherless on Tyneside.'

On the First Day of the Somme every one of the Tyneside Irish Battalions was reduced to about half their size. In total over 2,100 officers and men of the Tyneside Irish Brigade were either dead or wounded on that one fateful day.

All ranks of the 1/5th Battalion, Northumberland Fusiliers (T.F. cheering after the attack on Le Sars, near Albert, 7 October 191

Forgotten Battalions on the Somme

On the First Day of the Somme other battalions of The Northumberland Fusiliers, every one of them raised or containing men from Newcastle, were also present but not part of the advance, or they served in the later battles of the Somme that rolled on until November 1916. In so many ways these brave soldiers and the battles they fought have been overshadowed by the First Day and have been all but forgotten.

For example there was the 9th (Service) Battalion which contained the 'Quaysider' lads of 'B' Company who were in reserve with the rest of 17th (Northern) Division on 1 July 1916 but their time for action certainly came on 5 - 7 July in the bitter struggle for Quadrangle Trench. After the battalion was relieved and assembled near the cross roads south-west of Fricourt to reorganise and issue rum, rations and tabs they then set off in pouring rain to march to Meaulte where they would go into billets. After those recent days of fighting they left behind them 14 officers and 299 other ranks killed, wounded or missing.

The 10th and 11th Battalions were part of the 23rd Division and served in the battles for Albert, Bazentin

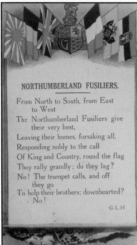

NORTHUMBERLAND FUSILIERS.

From North to South, from East
to West
The Northumberland Fusiliers give
their very best,
Leaving their homes, forsaking all,
Responding nobly to the call
Of King and Country, round the flag
They rally grandly; do they lag?
No! The trumpet calls, and off
they go
To help their brothers; downhearted?
No!

G.L.H

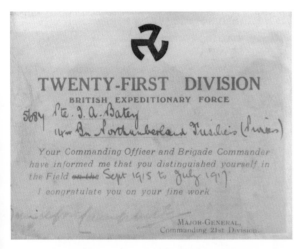

PLAYER'S CIGARETTES.

21ST DIVISION.

PLAYER'S CIGARETTES.

Above: One of the 18th Battalion, Northumberland Fusilier (Pioneers), 'Somewhere in France' 1916
Top left: Sgt Major G. Parfitt and Lieut. Peyton, 2 Platoon, A Company, 13th (Service) Battalion, Northumberland Fusiliers, Corbie, Somme 1916 with a fine tribute to the Northumberland Fusiliers on a First World War postcard.
Middle: A Divisional Commanders commendation card in recognition of distinguished conduct awarded to Pte. Batey of 14th (Service) Battalion, Northumberland Fusiliers (FMN) *Middle Right:* The insignia of the 21st Division – three red sevens joined at the centre.
Bottom: Northumberland Fusilier Pioneers photographed in the Somme in 1916 with some of their souvenirs, including a variety of German spiked helmets (FMN). *Bottom right:* Insignia of 50th (Northumbrian) Division

Ridge, Pozieres, Flers-Courcelette, The Battle of Morval, Le Transloy and the capture of Le Sars.

The 12th, 13th and 14th Battalions of Northumberland Fusiliers were all part of the 21st Division in the Fricourt sector of the Somme front from 1 July.

On the First Day the 12th Battalion were under orders to carry stores for the 63rd Infantry Brigade and to support for the attacking battalions as required. Although not part of the main advance the battalion suffered twenty-seven officers and men killed, 154 wounded and twenty-seven missing between 1-3 July.

The 13th Battalion, Northumberland Fusiliers had been split up into several parties to perform a number of duties on 1 July. Each company had three officers and 100 other ranks on detached duty attached to different Tunnelling and Field Companies of the, Royal Engineers and Officer Commanding 14 Northumberland Fusiliers (Pioneers) in the Becourt Valley. The remainder of the battalion consisting of Headquarters, Lewis Gunners, Company Bombers, Battalion Bombers and Signals were in Meaulte, from where they moved to occupy captured German trenches until 3 July carrying supplies and ammunition to the forward troops. Two squads of bombers and one Lewis gun were sent forward to hold up counter attacks that came on no less than three occasions from Fricourt Wood during the afternoon of 1 July.

The account of 'A' Company in the 13th Battalion War Diary paints a vivid picture of the sort of role of the men of all three battalions carried out over 1-3 July:

'A' Company (less company bombers) consisting of three Officers and 100 other ranks were ordered to cross 'No Man's Land as soon as our second objective had been gained and assist in the making of strong points in consolidating. The Company crossed 'No Man's Land' at 12.30 am on the night of 1-2 July. As the work of consolidation could not be done two parties were formed of 50 other ranks. One of these was sent forward with Stokes gun ammunition to Sunken Road where it was detained as support to 1/Lincoln Regt. On the 3rd July during the attack on Shelter Wood when reinforcements were called for to repel a counter attack this party was sent up under command of Sergeant R. Sinclair (the Officer Commanding the party having been previously wounded). The party outflanked the enemy on the right and captured thirty prisoners, they consolidated position gained in Shelter Wood and held on until relieved.

The other party of fifty was sent to and fro with rations and finally joined the battalion in Brandy Trench where work of consolidation was carried on. At 9.30am on July 3rd this party under their company commander moved up to Sunken Road was used for escorting prisoners and more especially for carrying up ammunition and bombs, food and water to the front line in Shelter Wood. Two squads of company bombers were sent as reinforcements to 'D' Company in Shelter Wood. Of these squads Cpl. Skinner volunteered to go out single handed over the open to endeavour to silence a machine gun that was holding up the advance of 'D' Company. He was with difficulty restrained and subsequently led his bombers round on the flank and silenced the gun.'

By such selfless acts of bravery, often unmarked, unrecorded and unrecognised gains in some corner of that foreign field were won.

The regular soldiers of the 1st Battalion had already cut their teeth up on the Ypres salient and distinguished themselves at the Battle of St. Eloi back in March 1916. They would fight on the Somme during the Battles for Albert, Bazentin and Delville Wood and saw out the

1916 campaign on Somme in the Battle of the Ancre.

The 4th-7th Territorial Force Battalions of the Northumberland Fusiliers were all part of 50th (Northumbrian) Division and had already made a name for themselves during the hard fighting around Ypres in 1915 before they joined the fighting on the Somme for the third offensive and the Battle of Flers Courcelette on 15 September 1916. It was a hard fought battle but one where many of our lads were fascinated and greatly encouraged by the sight for the first time in action of a new 'secret weapon' of the British – the tank. Then on they went through the Battle of Morval and to the Fourth Army's final offensive on the Somme, the Battle of the Transloy Ridges where they helped pave the way to the capture of Le Sars.

For the men of the Northumberland Fusilier's Pioneer Battalions such as the 17th, 18th or 19th Battalions or those that were attached to Divisions in pioneer roles such as the 7th or 14th Battalions; their war would be marked by hard marching and hard work under dangerous conditions for not only would they maintain supplies of ammunition, bombs food and equipment from forward dumps in battle areas and fill in fighting roles when needed, it also fell to them to dig trenches, pits for mortars and repair roads both under fire and within range of shells. Norman Gladden, of the 7th Battalion (who published a number of books on his experiences during the First World War), thought of the Pioneers rather like the pawns on a chess board because they could often be moved several times during the course of a day in battle, could be used to support, defend and attack and ultimately could be expendable.

Pte. T. Wilson of B Company, 18th Northumberland Fusiliers (Newcastle Pioneers) wrote of the Somme in his diary:

'I will never forget as long as I live and I think Tyneside will never forget too. We were in the attack from 1st July until 6th July, working both day and night without any sleep and just a hard biscuit every day to eat and bully beef and the sights we saw was heartbreaking to see and the smell of the dead was awful to stand. Every man worked like a lion every day 'til we got relieved on 6th July and mind it was a relieve to us all as we never had a wash nor a shave for six days and we were up to our knees in mud and our feet was very wet. We had to cut the socks off our feet with them being wet and muddy mixed...Just two days before we left the trenches we had to go all over the battle-field to gather the dead up and carry them to a certain place, lay them all side by side till we got a lot together before they buried them. I may tell you that both the smell and the sight was cruel to stand and see all the dead bodies all over.'

Northumberland Fusilier Territorial Battalion signallers, message carriers and runners serving in 50th (Northumbrian) Division, Somme, France 1916.

Aftermath and remembrance

As the tragic news of Tyneside's loss came home and page after page of the *Illustrated Chronicle* filled with the portraits of the fallen under such banners as heroes of 'The Great Advance' or 'The Harvest of Death on the Somme;' tragic rolls of honour recording the legions of the dead, the wounded and the missing appeared in every newspaper and thousands of local homes went into mourning but the war did not end on the Somme.

The Newcastle Commercials, Tyneside Scottish and Tyneside Irish battalions would all be rebuilt and would fight with distinction again. Reinforcements would come from their home county but with the lion's share being conscripts from all over the Britain it meant the character of the battalions would never be quite the same again. That said, the wry humour of the Tynesiders certainly remained. After the Battle of the Somme The Tyneside Scottish were granted a 'sandbag tartan' backing of a few inches square to be worn behind their Glengarry badges. When presented with this piece of fabric a good few of them pondered if they got this for going through that hellish battle what on earth did they have to do to get a whole kilt?

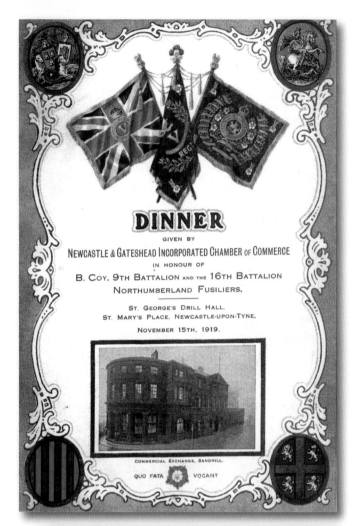

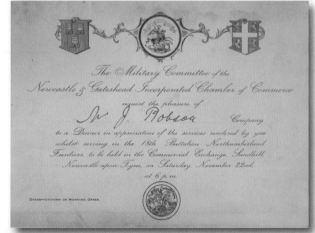

Top: Menu card for the celebration dinner held for the 9th and 16th Battalions, Northumberland Fusiliers at St. George's Drill Hall on 15 November 1919.
Right: Invitation to welcome home and give thanks to the men of the 18th Battalion, Northumberland Fusiliers (Pioneers) at the Commercial Exchange, Sandhill (FMN).

Top: 'The Response' monument erected to commemorate the raising of 'B' Company, 9th Battalion and the 16th, 18th and 19th Service Battalions, Northumberland Fusiliers by the Newcastle & Gateshead Chamber of Commerce commissioned by Sir George and Lady Renwick in thankfulness for the safe return of their five sons from the war, it was unveiled by the Prince of Wales in 1923. *Top right:* The Newcastle War Memorial in Old Eldon Square, unveiled by Field Marshal Sir Douglas Haig in 1923. *Right:* Memorial to the fallen of the 6th (Newcastle) Battalion, Northumberland Fusiliers erected in 1924 *Above:* The reverse of 'The Response' showing the dedication of the memorial.

Select Bibliography and a note on sources

Brewis, Alfred *The Northumberland Fusiliers (The Fighting Fifth)* (Newcastle 1915)

Buckley, Captain Francis, *Q.6.A and other places. Recollections of 1916,1917,1918* (London 1920)

Buckley, Captain Francis (ed.) *War History of the 7th Northumberland Fusiliers* (Newcastle 1919)

Cantlie, James *First Aid to the Injured* (London 1915)

Chappell, Mike *The Somme 1916: Crucible of a British Army* (1998)

Cooke, Capt. C. H. *Historical Records of the 9th (Service) Battalion Northumberland Fusiliers* (Newcastle 1928)

Cooke, Capt. C. H. *Historical Records of the 16th (Service) Battalion Northumberland Fusiliers* (Newcastle 1923)

Cooke, Capt. C. H. *Historical Records of the 19th (Service) Battalion Northumberland Fusiliers* (Newcastle 1920)

Farrah-Hockley, Anthony *The Somme* (New Edition, London 1999)

Gladden, Norman *The Somme 1916: A Personal Account* (London 1974)

Johnson, Ian *Newcastle Commercials, 16th (Service) Battalion Northumberland Fusiliers* (Newcastle 2016)

Lavery, Felix (comp.) Keating, Joseph and O'Connor, T. P. *Irish Heroes in the War* (London 1917)

Macdonald, Lyn *Somme* (London 1983)

Middlebrook, Martin *The First Day on the Somme* (London 1971)

Parker, Peter *The Old Lie* (London 1987)

Reader, W. J., *At Duty's Call: A Study in Obsolete Patriotism* (Manchester 1988)

Sandilands, Brig. H. R. *Fifth in the Great War: A History of the 1st and 2nd Northumberland Fusiliers, 1914-1918* (Dover 1938)

Sellwood, A. V., *The Saturday Night Soldiers* (London 1966)

Shakespear, Lt. Col. John *Historical Records of the 17th (Service) Battalion Northumberland Fusiliers (N.E.R. Pioneers)* (Newcastle 1926)

Shakespear, Lt. Col. John *Historical Records of the 18th (Service) Battalion Northumberland Fusiliers* (Pioneers) (Newcastle 1920)

Sheen, John *Tyneside Irish 24th, 25th & 26th & 27th (Service) Battalions of the Northumberland Fusiliers* (Barnsley 1998)

Simkins, Peter *Kitchener's Army: The Raising of the New Armies 1914-1916* (Barnsley 2007)

Stewart, Graham and Sheen, John *Tyneside Scottish: 20th, 21st, 22nd and 23rd (Service) Battalions of the Northumberland Fusiliers* (Barnsley 1998)

Storey, Neil R., *The Tommy's Handbook* (Stroud 2014)

Storey, Neil R., *Women in the First World War* (Shire 2010)

Ternan, Brig-Gen. Trevor *The Story of the Tyneside Scottish* (Newcastle 1919)

Westlake, Ray *British Battalions on the Somme* (Barnsley 1994)

Westlake, Ray *Kitcheners Army* (Tunbridge Wells 1989)

Westlake, Ray *The Territorial Battalions* (London 1986)

Reference Books and Official Publications

Kelly's Directory of Durham and Northumberland
(London 1914)
*Soldiers Died in the Great War: Northumberland
Fusiliers* (HMSO 1921)
*War Office, Scheme for the Organisation of Voluntary
Aid in England and Wales* (HMSO 1909)

Newspapers, Journals and Magazines

Evening Chronicle (Newcastle)
Family Tree Magazine
Illustrated Chronicle (Newcastle)
Illustrated War News
Shields Daily News
St. Georges Gazette
The Colliery Guardian
The Growler
The Newcastle Daily Journal
The Northerner
The Rutherfordian
The Times
*Transactions of The North of England Institute of
Mining and Mechanical Engineers*
War Illustrated

War Diaries

War Diaries of all the active service battalions of the
Northumberland Fusiliers can be found on Microfiche
at Newcastle Central Library, Local Studies.

A few of the simple wooden crosses that marked the graves of fallen Northumberland Fusiliers on the Somme.

'Some corner of a foreign field, that is forever England.'